Rudolf Steiner Education
and the Developing Child

Rudolf Steiner Education
and the Developing Child

Willi Aeppli

Anthroposophic Press

This volume is a translation of *Aus der Unterrichtspraxis an einer Rudolf Steiner Schule* published by Zbinden Verlag, Basel, 1970. German copyright © by Aya Haerri-Aeppli. The translation was made by Angelika V. Ritscher-Hill.

10 9 8 7 6 5 4 3

Library of Congress Cataloging-in-Publication Data

Aeppli, Willi, 1894–1972.
   Rudolf Steiner education and the developing child.

   Translation of: Aus der Unterrichtspraxis an
einer Rudolf Steiner Schule.
   Bibliography.
   1. Waldorf method of education.   2. Education—
Philosophy.   3. Child development.   I. Title.
LB1029.W34A3713   1986   370'.1   86-10864
ISBN 0-88010-164-4

Printed in the United States of America

Contents

Translator's Preface

Although much has been written about education and educating, there is always an aspect or approach that is fresh and exciting. This book is a prime example. Willi Aeppli, an experienced teacher in the system known as Rudolf Steiner or Waldorf Education, allows us to enter his classroom—we hear the children speak, we see their little faces, and we remember for a while what it was like to be eight years old. Through his children we gain insights that serve as invaluable guides not only for educators, but also for adults in general.

On a more personal level, I chose to translate this work for two reasons: First, because I, myself, went through all twelve grades in Waldorf Schools. I began with the Waldorf School on Long Island, moved on to the Green Meadow School in Spring Valley, New York and Michael Hall in England, and finished with the Rudolf Steiner School in New York City. Having been on the receiving end, as it were, for so many years, it was of particular interest to me to learn what it was like standing on the other side of the desk. Second, Aeppli's book was recommended to me by a teacher at the Green Meadow School, for whom it continues to be an inspiration. This can hold true for all of us, but it may first be necessary to clarify certain terms with which Aeppli assumes we are familiar. I will therefore take this opportunity to say a few explanatory words.

Perhaps the most frequent term that appears is "Anthroposophy" ("wisdom of man"), a philosophy that imbues Waldorf Education, but is under no circumstances taught in the schools. The point is not for the teacher to indoctrinate the children with his own personal convictions, but to allow Anthroposophy to awaken in him the proper educational forces. Thus, it is not Anthroposophy itself which needs to be discussed here, but Waldorf Education in the light of Anthroposophy.

The essence of the Waldorf method is the belief that education is an art. Whatever the subject, its presentation to the child must live—it must speak to the child's experience. Educating the whole child means addressing the forces of his mind, his heart and his will. A "main lesson" forms the cornerstone upon which the child's day is built. It is an uninterrupted, two-hour period at the beginning of each school day, in which a single subject (literature, geometry, botany, etc.) is studied in three- to six-week blocks. Waldorf schools try to make each day an organic whole. Since people are generally more awake and alert in the morning, the subjects requiring knowledge and understanding are taught first. Reading and writing at various levels are practiced in connection with the subject of the lesson. Later in the morning come the subjects requiring regular rhythmic repetition, such as foreign languages, music and gym. The day ends with activities such as arts and crafts, gardening or scientific experiments, which require manual dexterity. Thus, each school day has a rhythm of head, heart and hands, of inner and outer activity.

As the child goes through certain phases of development, so do the subjects. The teacher, together with the parents, shares the responsibility for shaping the child with the proper mixture of authority and respect for the child's individuality. The goal is to send young adults into the world who can stand on their own two feet, and who can accept responsibility for their own actions.

One point of clarification before discussing problems of

translation: In Waldorf schools the children are taught certain speech exercises in which the vowels are pronounced phonetically as *ah, eh, ee, oh,* and *ooh.* Similarly, when the children are taught eurythmy (a rhythmic form of dance to music and gesture) these same sounds are used, only now in combination with a gesture, as seen in Plate 1.

As far as the translation itself is concerned, I faced only one major problem. The author provides us with two pages of wonderful illustrations that show how a teacher could introduce the children to the letters of the alphabet. The letter H, for instance, is introduced in a story involving a hare. Since the German word for hare is *Hase,* the translation for this particular word presented no problem. When we are dealing with a giant, however, for which the German word is *Riese,* an obvious difficulty arises. I therefore took the liberty of altering or replacing the original pictures or of changing the original story, where necessary.

A minor problem was caused by the German use of three more or less interchangeable words for "teacher": *Lehrer, Erzieher, Pädagoge.* I chose to translate all these words primarily with teacher, although on a few occasions the word educator seemed more appropriate.

Throughout the book I was faced with dozens of direct quotations from various authors, for which the source works were rarely given. Where possible I located the source work myself and have indicated it with the appropriate footnote. Unfortunately, however, my research often proved futile, and many quotations had to be left as they appeared in the original text, without source reference. The most frequent quotations were taken from works by the educator Paul Vital Troxler, which I found impossible to obtain even by means of an inter-library search. Although I met with greater success in locating works by Johann Heinrich Pestalozzi, another great educator, some quotations still remain unidentified. Should a reader decide to pursue the search further, it will save him some time to know that the relevant passages by Pestalozzi are not to be found in *The Education of Man, How Gertrude Teaches Her Children,* and *My Life and Experiences.*

In conclusion, I would like to take this opportunity to acknowledge with thanks the invaluable help given me by my father, H. Jan Ritscher. Without his wealth of knowledge about Anthroposophy I would have been unable to do justice to Mr. Aeppli's inspiring work.

Angelika V. Ritscher-Hill
March, 1985

Preface to the First Edition

The following twelve essays on education were written over the course of seven years when, as a teacher at the Rudolf Steiner School in Basel, Switzerland, I was entrusted with guiding a group of children from the first through the seventh grade. These essays relate the experiences and insights granted me by the children themselves at each stage of their development and in every new subject.

In reading this book, the experienced teacher will realize, I hope, that I am not simply theorizing on the ideal of a good education. Everything written here, as the title of this book indicates, is the result of a variety of practical experiences.

These essays appeared in "Menschenschule" (School for Mankind), a monthly journal for education and teacher training published by C. Englert-Faye. Some of them were first presented as lectures that I held in Basel and Zurich. In writing these down, I retained the lecture format unless doing so would have distracted the reader.

Basel, March 1934
Willi Aeppli

Preface to the Second Edition

Sixteen years after this book was first published, a new edition has proved necessary. Its form remains the same, as I saw no reason to make changes in the text. Let me take this opportunity, however, to inform the reader that a second volume of "Teaching Experiences" will appear in the near future.

Basel, October 1950
Willi Aeppli

Sense and Nonsense in Education

Education invariably involves two quite distinct people. On the one hand, the teacher, in other words, a particular adult, with insights and blind spots, strengths and weaknesses, and thousands of abilities and inabilities. On the other hand, there is an equally concrete being, namely a particular child (not simply *the* child as meaningless abstraction), with gifts and potentials all waiting to be realized and transformed into outward abilities. This child, however, is not equipped to walk the path leading to true humanity on his own. He depends on the daily help of the adults to whom destiny has led him. He is helpless before these adults and entrusts them with his future for better or for worse.

Seen in this light, every child appears to be at a disadvantage in comparison to other beings such as animals. Unlike the young child, the young *animal* is not totally helpless. It is born with the wisdom and strength to survive, and it can use them at an early age, often as soon as a few days after birth. It is born an almost finished being, needing to make only a small leap into full adulthood. It thereby escapes the necessity of being raised.

This seeming disadvantage of the child, however, represents the only possibility for his gradual development into a *human* being. As the animal is completely developed at birth, it is denied the opportunity of being raised. In other words, it is cut off from the possibility of development. At best it can become a creature trained by man. Such training, however, goes against animal nature and has nothing to do with human education; it is mere conditioning. True enough, if man were also completely developed at birth, he would no longer have to be raised, but life would then be an automatic process solely determined by destiny and the laws of nature. There would be no room for human freedom or for actions based on insight.

Fortunately, human beings are born incomplete in every way, and education can help transform destiny into freedom. But every adult in a child's environment represents destiny, a stroke of good or bad fortune, which will have a decisive influence on that child's life. Although the child brings all his human talents to earth as a divine gift, he cannot develop them for later use without "outside" help. Only an adult, who becomes his destiny, can help him find himself. For the adult, however, each child who enters his life represents a responsibility, and one that cannot be avoided. No one can say that he is never involved with children. A child speaks to me. My answer, and the way I give it, has a fateful impact on that child. Beyond the substance of my response, the answer can express goodwill, impatience, anger or nervousness, all of which the child takes in. In fact, I need not even speak to the child in words, so in tune is he with my entire being, faults and all. The primary characteristic of every child is receptiveness.

Education still does not concern me, claims a particularly stubborn individual. That same evening, however, he goes for a walk in the woods and is promptly attacked. He is definitely the victim of his assailant's poor education, and he has the bruises to show for it. Now, consider the case of a certain mass-murderer, one Mr. Kürten, whose brain, when dissected after death, was found to be constructed normally. How lucky for the conscience of mankind! Had his brain been structurally abnormal, everyone would have blamed the diseased brain, instead of himself or Kürten, for the crimes committed. As it is, the question of conscience remains inescapable: How can a human being commit such horrible deeds? Could proper education perhaps have prevented this? Kürten himself gave the judge the answer to these questions, which, although widely reported by the media, was nevertheless disregarded. Kürten said: "If just once, when I was still a child, someone had said a kind word to me, none of this would have happened." Kürten's misfortune was that as a child not one adult addressed the humanness, the higher self in him; he thus had to become subhuman.

Education concerns everyone. The responsibility of being a teacher arises in everyone's life, and this responsibility cannot be completely fobbed off on those trained in education. It is a matter which concerns every individual, without exception.

What then is the essence of education, we ask ourselves. Is it primarily to nurture and harden the physical body? Is it to cram the child with the maximum number of facts? Is it to mold the child into a carbon copy of his teacher? Or is it, perhaps, something quite different?

Some hundred and fifty years ago and in the same country, two great educators, Heinrich Pestalozzi and Paul Vital Troxler, were at work. Imagine that a teacher, guided by his better instincts, discovers these two educators. He might, for example, stumble onto Troxler's words on the essence of education:

> He who puts himself in someone else's hands to be educated offers the greatest possible sacrifice, namely himself, all his gifts, and his entire future. He therefore has the right to demand that through the teacher his self be returned to him. Indeed, the condition of this apparent self-relinquishment is that he become stronger and true to himself, so that he may live out his original, natural

destiny and his freedom of choice more securely and happily. Thus, education should neither give nor take, but simply guide man back to his true nature, which, in turn, is revealed only by his liberated education. Education is the revelation of the creator's divine love for the human race. Only God can truly teach, and true education is nothing but releasing and freeing. There is more at stake here than mere earthly life and routine existence, more than mere property, liberty and honor.

This is the clear expression of the purpose of education. A child should be led to himself through education. This education should neither give nor take, but only bring to fullest possible fruition what is sown in each child, each in a unique way, as a gift from God.

Certain questions can be raised here, such as, Are not these words simply idle chatter? And does not education, when stripped of rhetoric, simply mean teaching the maximum number of facts, to be regurgitated when needed? The teacher must also be prepared for the question, Is it not best to ignore the self of the child, which is an eternal mystery anyway, and do everything to instill in the child, as the highest goal (even above facts), our own Weltanschauung? An outlook, which has been formed over the years into a well-founded "opinion" on all aspects of the world? Is it not imperative to teach the child a belief (meaning my belief), whether it be religious, political or scientific?

Such questions lead us to the opposite of true education, namely to the nonsense of drilling and conditioning.

No one can refute my argument that the primary purpose of education today, at least in Europe, consists in cramming the child full of an immense stock of facts, from which it can draw for the rest of his life. That is why these facts are still meticulously tested year after year. The teaching material becomes important in itself because the child must be able to present it on command. The subject matter is no longer a means to an end, but an end in itself, and the student is judged according to how much he knows. Taken to extremes, this is no longer education, but, to paraphrase Nietzsche, the creation of a walking, talking dictionary. Does school-knowledge as determined by exams, have anything at all to do with becoming a human being? In other words, does that kind of knowledge prepare the child for life's challenges? It is not unusual for an individual with the most advanced academic degrees to find himself incapable of coping with life's most basic demands, even though he has successfully completed his exams and possesses vast knowledge. Withdrawn from the real world, he must be cared for in a quiet, protected place.

The "maximum number" in terms of facts also implies "maximum speed." So many reforms in education prove to be, at closer look, only more sophisticated methods of teaching the child even faster than before. A child should now reach in one stride, what he could once, for his own well-being, approach more slowly. Thus, if a five-year-old boy learns to read perfectly in four weeks, the feat is broadcast to the world as successful education, when it is in reality no more than successful rote learning. The goal of "education" in this instance, is to turn a child into an adult as quickly as possible. The ideal education creates the miniature grown-up, even if he is only eight years old. The child has no sooner stepped into the classroom than a force is addressed that would prefer to unfold gradually. This force, an adult characteristic, is the intellect. It is awakened too soon, and the child, contrary to God's plan, is thrown prematurely into adulthood. What is natural for the animal is unnatural for the child. The animal rushes headlong into full growth, skipping the childhood stage and leaping into animal completeness. But it is a leap into the lower nature, away from humanness.

A curriculum that is directed to the intellectual forces of the children too early and too one-sidedly means, once again in extreme terms, training children to be no more than intellectual animals or, according to Pestalozzi, "reasoning beasts." Troxler, however, says the following about curricular content:

> [The number and choice of subjects may not be determined by the principle of usefulness. He who proceeds from this utilitarian, egotistical point of view], loses the man who lives for himself, as well as for higher purposes, to the slave of routine, . . . he will bury his human spirit . . . under an enormous mountain of superficial facts and skills. He may win the world, but he will lose his soul. On the other hand, he who sees the outer materials and forms that are presented as school subjects only as a means to educate and exercise man's soul forces, . . . for him the very diversity of their application will make the great work [of human education] possible.

There is yet another opposing view of true education. Put into words, it could sound like this: Control young people and you control the future. This is diametrically opposed to Troxler's idea that "education is only a releasing and freeing." Here speaks the teacher, there the seducer and destroyer. Here education is rooted in itself and in the nature of man, there "education" is means to an end that lies beyond the individual man. It is, therefore, no longer education, but an indoctrination in a particular Weltanschauung, be it a party line, religious dogma or other opinion on world affairs.

What does the statement, control young people and you control the future, actually mean? If I want my own Weltanschauung, and the power it gave me, to be preserved as long as possible, and if I want its influence to be felt after I am gone, then I must address the next generation, impressing upon them my view of how things should be run. Education then becomes a means of preserving a belief that may once have been valid for an individual or a group of people. This means, however, that the teacher is no longer struggling to develop the humanness in the child, nor is he helping the forces in the child that wait to be released and freed. Instead he is trying to use young people as power pawns; he is struggling for possession of the next generation.

And yet, it is a fundamental insight that the purpose of education is not to preserve the present, but to prepare for the future.

Somebody might say at this point, I do not want my children, or those children entrusted to me, to preserve the present. I am very dissatisfied with the present. I do, however, dream of an exceptionally beautiful and ideal future that I hope the children can realize one day the way I envision it. As a teacher, am I not serving humanity that way? Perhaps this person is a convinced pacifist, or nationalist, or communist, or reformist—it really makes no difference when it comes to beautiful and ideal futures. "I do not wish," he says, "to abuse my power over the child in order to preserve the present. I desire only to see the child realize the ideal I have in mind."

We must have no illusions on this score. If the adult is speaking of the future as he imagines it, then this future is simply part of his Weltanschauung. After all, it does not live in his limbs or in his entire being. It is a mental picture, and since he likes this picture, he mistakenly believes it lives in his heart. Pictures of the future when presented in book form are called utopias, and many of these books have been published. All pictures of man's future are utopias. Each one is legitimate only for the person who envisioned it in his mind, and only for the present, not for a distant future.

Where does the future live not as Fata Morgana, but as

reality? I believe, in every human being! The future lives quite concretely in every child, but not as a thought up, planned out, yearned for and dreamed about ideal. It is something very real, albeit nascent and uncertain (visible from the outside only in the child's constantly growing body) in the child's physical, soul and spirit bodies.

The child wants to grow more than just physically. He will forge a new present one day, which will look completely different from the way any adult could have imagined. If we do not see, or divine, this reality in children, and instead try to teach them to reach for our shadowy picture of the future, then we cheat them out of the future which is rightfully theirs. By imposing our existence on the child, we stifle his inner development. We give the child a picture or a dogma, and take away his future, to which he has a legitimate claim.

There is a revolutionary aspect to education that we must not forget. Education is an insurrection, a rebellion. That which is developing confronts that which has already become; the future confronts the past, and man's true progress consists of the legitimate future triumphing over, or actually fulfilling, the outdated past in a legitimate way. Yet the forces which arise to forge a new present as fulfillment of the past have nothing to do with terror or violence. Troxler expresses this as follows:

> A proper and planned insurrection works through education, and education that does not consistently raise the majority of students above the cultural level of the human race during their teachers' generation, is poor, illegitimate, and sounding its own death knell . . . That which actively opposes the insurrection I mentioned, is revolutionary in the bad sense of the word.

What happens if the present, which is instantly the past, is arbitrarily preserved through "education"? One possibility is that those robbed of their future will give up, become weaklings, moral cowards or insecure individuals because they will be unable to find themselves. If they are stronger-willed, they may be forced into an unproductive rebellion against the world at large, precisely because they were not allowed to participate in the natural insurrection. They fight everything, but it is really a fight against something inside themselves which is not their self, but a foreign element which prevents their self from finding itself.

If in order to preserve the present for another generation the children are conditioned for that present, without taking their future into proper consideration, then that present becomes corrupted. The corruption destroys all life forces, and petrification occurs. Such is the present situation if we see it without blinders, and unsuccessful education is to blame. True human education can cure what has become diseased. The words of Pestalozzi are valid still:

> The morally, spiritually and socially oppressed part of this world can be saved only through education; through the education of humanness; through the cultural shaping of mankind.

Over a hundred and fifty years ago Pestalozzi and Troxler called attention to tasks that have never been carried out. They must be taken on again today.

But let us now return to the concept of true education which is identical with the idea of the cultural shaping of mankind. Here the authorized parts ways with the unauthorized. On construction sites, in offices, factories and a host of other locations we often read the warning: Authorized personnel only. How much more apropos is this warning for a school, where the human spirit is cultivated. Though no one can say education does not concern him, that fact alone does not give him the inner authority to have a say in the matter. Authority cannot be given. It can be gained only by personal, inner striving.

What, then, is involved in becoming an authority on education? First, the demands made on the teacher by life's realities, and not by some external authority. Everything depends on whether the teacher feels these demands not as a categorical imperative from the outside to which he must yield, but as something that he *wants* to do, even quite on his own, out of natural inclination.

Second, if he wishes to be authorized to teach, the teacher must learn to approach the subject material in freedom, rather than losing his soul to it.

Third, the teacher must learn to recognize of his own free will that something which he considers part of himself, namely his Weltanschauung, is his own personal conviction. As a teacher, he must not cling to lofty ideals, hobbies, programs or doctrines. As long as he teaches, he must be able to still all these voices. But this is possible only if he has the strength to see beyond them.

He should even learn to face his intellect and to still its voice as well should the teaching situation warrant it.

What is thus revealed as a necessity for the teacher? A *philosophy of freedom*, not as a theory, philosophical system of concepts, or Weltanschauung, but as a way of life, a capacity.

If the purpose of education is not to give or take, but simply to strengthen the forces inherent in the child's self, then the teacher must be able to recognize that self in each child. He must search for a real psychology with which to perceive how that self is shaped and articulated, what transformations it is undergoing, and how it can be both recognized and supported. Through such a psychology, which should not be mere system or theory, he must be alert to the diverse outward manifestations of these soul forces in a child.

The real meaning of the teaching material leads the

teacher away from the child to the world as a whole, to earth and sky, to stone, plant and animal, to the individual, as well as to all of mankind. Real world knowledge is now required. If Weltanschauung consists of opinions and desires (composed of formulas, programs, dogmas and doctrines) regarding the world and how it operates, then world knowledge arises out of contemplative powers of judgment. Such a goal is reached by a longer path.

The demands upon a teacher are great. Is he capable of meeting them, even partially?

We established at the beginning of this book that every adult has some responsibility for teaching. He cannot shirk this sacred responsibility since he cannot banish children from his environment. He is free only to succeed or fail in his responsibility. There is also a positive side to this imposed responsibility: it allows the adult to educate himself. The possibility of self-education balances out the necessity of teaching and of being taught. Contrary to popular belief, education and self-education have nothing to do with a greater or lesser amount of knowledge. In essence they have much more to do with releasing and freeing, sometimes working outwards from myself on others, sometimes working inwards on myself through myself. Self-education is possible, however, only if we are not lazy. The possibility of self-education is a divine gift, which we are free to use or not. Without self-education, however, we cannot realize our own humanity. This is the foundation on which all education rests—the more we realize our humanity, the greater our power to educate. Now we can understand Troxler when he says: *"Self-education is divine."*
And Pestalozzi's words as well: *"Every developed human force is in itself a truly moral force."*

The possibility of self-education is at the same time the only possibility of education. We can teach only with human forces, developed through inner work, for they alone are moral. The teacher who does not take advantage of this possibility succumbs to the nonsense of drilling and conditioning.

How does the present look for each one of us? Where are the forces which make it possible for me to truly teach, by allowing me to touch the souls of the children? If I am honest with myself, I must admit that I lack these entirely, and that my words and deeds do not reach the innermost being of a child. I must come to the uncomfortable, but fundamental and perhaps fruitful conclusion, that I can do a great deal with the forces I have at my disposal, namely the forces of the intellect. With the intellect I can theorize, systematize, register, categorize, observe the world in a rational way and create my own beautiful Weltanschauung. I can be a great success in my everyday life. There is only one thing that I definitely cannot do, and that is teach. If I rely only on this one force, then I will have nothing to draw on in my teaching situations, for the teaching instincts of previous generations will also be dead in me. My teaching will be purely mechanical.

As we all know, the emptier the keg, the louder the tone when struck. Similarly, the emptier a man is on the inside, the greater his activity on the outside. Why is educational science so highly developed? Because we have such a highly developed intellect. Why are all aspects of our educational curriculum so weak? Because we cannot understand education with our intellect. Not even the most sophisticated educational science is much use. The teacher must develop creative abilities which he may not even know he has, so tightly are they ensnared in the cobweb of intellectual thinking. Education cannot be a science, only an art. Art, however, comes from ability.

To come to such a realization, and to suffer from it, is the first step forward, for it is the first step towards self-awareness. Out of our self-awareness comes the insight of how necessary it is to transform thinking that merely categorizes and structures into thinking that is alive and active— thinking which at first is creative only in a modest way, but eventually makes contact with life's realities possible. Realities, however, are always living processes. Thus, the transformation of thinking would mean breaking through the intellect to one's own essence and humanity; it would represent the first steps on a path toward an anthroposophy. Creating an anthroposophy, not as a philosophical system, but as a living knowledge of man and the world was what, for example, Troxler endeavored to achieve. Approximately one hundred and fifty years ago, he said the following in his Bernese lecture series:

> There is no doubt that this [true] philosophy is founded on a higher, inner . . . consciousness, I would say, on a self-conscious, freely achieved clairvoyance, which reunites the most profound, innermost sight with external consciousness and reasoning. This inner consciousness is the source of all inspirations and all creative ideas.
>
> The [true] philosophy, however, is in its origin and perfection nothing other than anthroposophy, nothing other than the inspiration and completion of intelligence, consciousness and the knowledge of the human spirit in its entire scope, content, breadth and depth.
>
> This philosophical thinking as highest spiritual inner sight is the recreation of true education.

Paul Vital Troxler's anthroposophy and that of Rudolf Steiner are not two different things called by the same name. What Troxler saw distinctly and clearly as an idea, was realized by Rudolf Steiner. This anthroposophy, however, cannot be adopted as just another Weltanschauung. It has meaning only when it is realized anew by each individual to the best of his ability.

Rudolf Steiner wrote his *Philosophy of Freedom* in 1894. It fulfills Troxler's demand for a true philosophy. It is not an abstract, speculative system of concepts, but rather a path which can lead to inner sight. Through the *Philosophy*, the path to the creative human spirit is opened, for it teaches us how to think in a way entirely free of the senses. The human spirit is buried under illusory existences, held back by forces which do not express the purely human and which rob man of his freedom. Through the *Philosophy of Freedom* man gradually sees the extent to which he lives, and must continue to live, in unfreedom. He becomes aware of the motives for his actions: why he acted, or is forced to act, in a particular way. He is driven into action from two quite different directions. First, the inner drives, passions, and fanatical beliefs, which rise up out of his unfree being, clouding his consciousness and urging him to act. None of them, however, has anything to do with the true, inner essence of the individual. They are not the expression of the unique and immortal individuality, but only of the generic characteristics that he shares with all mankind. They tell us only that through them we belong to the "species man."

Second, there are the demands of custom, including moral codes, conventions, statutes, external laws and regulations, with which man is bombarded from the outside. By confronting him with an authoritative "you shall!" they all cause man to act. For one person it may be a political party that constantly directs his actions. For another it may be the pressure of "public opinion." Even if all these things were justified, they still would not come close to touching the innermost core of an individual, for they are entirely collective and normative and do not express the unique individual. Man may act properly and, so to speak, correctly as a result of these external factors, but he is acting neither out of his inner self nor freely.

Any instance in which man does not act freely, but only as species man or as the result of "herd" pressures, becomes part of a net of external existence around him. Should he knowledgeably search beyond this existence, he will encounter his actual inner being, which is not an existence, but a force. The external existence has no creative power. At best it can preserve what already exists. It cannot forge anything new. Rudolf Steiner says the following on this subject:

> Man is free in so far as he is able to obey himself in every moment of his life . . . Which of us can say that he is really free in all his actions? Yet in each of us there dwells a deeper being in which the free man finds expression . . . Indeed, we are men in the true sense only in so far as we are free . . . Nature makes of man merely a natural being, society makes of him a law-abiding being; only *he himself* can make of himself a *free man.* [1]

A free man creates his own motives for action. He then acts out of inclination and love, because the motive arises out of his original, true being. It is innately creative and moral. Rudolf Steiner called this force "moral imagination." Who needs it more than the teacher?

These are just a few thoughts from the *Philosophy of Freedom*, but studying them can be of great value to the teacher.

It becomes increasingly clear that the *Philosophy of Freedom* is a serious matter of consciousness, which can gradually lead to inner trials. Before this consciousness, a greater or lesser amount of knowledge is meaningless. This consciousness concerns the core of man, for it is this core which should be addressed. Something within ourselves should transform itself. The first effect of this self-transformation is that we regain trust in ourselves and in the still buried human spirit.

That trust also extends to the human spirit in other men, which need only be called upon to become effective. More clearly than before we see the inhumanity in ourselves and in others. It confronts us either in rigid standards or in the form of the entire animal kingdom. But we can also see beyond it and may be able to address what is purely human in other men.

It is the greatness of Troxler and Pestalozzi that they clearly perceived the not-yet-human, and yet never lost their trust in the individual himself. It was their profound belief that the source of all morality and the creator of all human culture is the individual human spirit. Out of this insight and this trust in the individual they drew the strength for their pedagogical work.

The prerequisite of all education is trust in the divine-human forces in the child. Without this trust, teaching is mere drilling and conditioning for a skill, or, perhaps, a doctrine.

A teacher who attempts to put a "philosophy of freedom" into practice the way of Pestalozzi and Troxler would have, finds himself on the path to his own humanity. He feels capable of helping the children make free use of their forces in later years, so that they can fulfill their free goals and destined purposes. He respects the gift of humanity in each child, without making the mistake of seeing them as adults, and becomes less and less prone to the nonsense of drilling. Only someone who is not striving to become free himself can wish a state of nonfreedom on others.

That teacher also knows that education and freedom do not mean teaching children to be egotistical. He knows that human spirits have a common source, and that the essence of the human spirit is tolerance. He sees egotism, on the other hand, as related to the outer existence of man.

Though these ideas may sound new, they were actually expressed over 150 years ago. Pestalozzi says, for example:

All men are in essence the same. Therefore the truth which is drawn purely from our innermost being will be the general truth of humanity.

How can we teach people to be social beings? By trying to perceive and nurture the child's innermost being, his self. This truly human individuality, worlds apart from any form of egotism, finds the way to other individuals, for all men, though of different stations, professions, nationalities and races are still of the same spirit.

The drives, passions, jealousies and fanatical beliefs welling up out of man's lower nature inevitably pit everyone against everyone else. All moral codes, conventions, treaties and pacts will be too weak to stem that devastating tide. What would be left to salvage and rebuild can come only out of the realm of the free human spirit. Calling up this human spirit in oneself is a matter of self-education. It can occur in adults only as a result of free will. The teacher who has become aware of his spirit experiences this spiritual law as an unbending truth.

Man can be forced to do a great deal as a result of external pressure. He can fill his head with facts, make good grades, acquire external skills, make great strides professionally, become a model soldier and a hundred other useful things, but he cannot be forced to educate himself. There is a point beyond which force no longer forces, and commands are powerless; a point beyond which instincts and passions no longer clamor for action. Beyond this point the human I reigns, and any activity arises solely out of self-knowledge, inclination and, above all, out of free choice.

True education is possible only through self-education. Whether he educates himself or extends a guiding hand to children, the teacher acts out of the same freedom. Both involve the innermost nature of man or, as Pestalozzi says, the individuality.

For the teacher to help the child in a truly educational way, he must use his own freely awakened forces. No one can order or forbid these forces, which are valuable only for education. It is just as impossible to submit them to an examination and evaluate them on a scale of A–F. Can an expert evaluate the strength of an applicant's moral forces? It is nevertheless these very forces on which teaching depends. They are intangible, but then education consists of many intangibles.

Out of such insights Troxler once dared to say the following:

The spirit, however, as all living things, stays only where earth and air ensure it an undisturbed self-development.

To Gügler:

I still dare to claim publicly, even in these times, that what you call church and state have no authority over the school system or the education of man.

The school is a living being and a well-structured organism and cannot be determined by decrees and experiments. Its makeup is a force of nature and ideas.

Free is that education which strives to be purely human in all subjects, and which in this striving neither incurs nor endures interference from the outside. [Such educational freedom] will not be blocked by any state regulation or constitution, for this freedom is an essential requirement and a basic condition of the republic. Nowhere does a citizen feel more human than in free nations, and nowhere else does he have a greater responsibility, as well as right, to be a human being.

Only this radical revolution in the school system, in your compatriots, in your most human citizens, can release and free you.

Rudolf Steiner's *Philosophy of Freedom* is the basis of his anthroposophy, and as such is already anthroposophy itself.

It is not, however, a Weltanschauung that can be adopted as simply as any other. It is a method of knowledge and therefore a "path," not a system. What does anthroposophy become when it turns toward the developing man, the child? It becomes a real psychology and pedagogy, but again not as a psychological system, but as a "method." Anthroposophy becomes a method of education which each individual teacher must recreate in himself and adapt to the inner and outer situation in which he finds himself. It is a path by which the teacher can awaken his teaching forces. But it is a path of self-education. Rudolf Steiner's pedagogical lectures and writings are of particular help along this path. They present in concrete detail the evolutionary stages through which a child must pass. These metamorphoses, the result of exact research, are not simply new facts at the teacher's disposal. They are means by which he may awaken to the children in his environment. Anthroposophy is actually just another word for "Awakening." Rudolf Steiner once said:

> Waldorf school education is not a pedagogical system, at all, but an art, so that what exists in man is awakened. Actually, Waldorf education does not even want to educate, but to awaken, for that is what we are dealing with today, awakening. First the teachers must be awakened, then the teachers must awaken the children and young people.

Education is releasing and freeing, says Troxler, and the same can be said of self-education. According to today's theory, however, the teacher must take a barrage of exams, and he in turn must submit the children to exams, as if anything significant were done for education that way.

Through Anthroposophy as psychology, the teacher is presented with new opportunities to get closer to the children. Gradually he gains a living insight into the individual child. He becomes concretely, and not just theoretically, aware of the life metamorphoses of the children. To take just one example out of many, he sees what transformations take place in those forces in the child which appear as intellectual capacity in the ten-year-old. He experiences them now as the result of a long development, and he himself has developed the inner strength to delay many aspects of education until these forces have become available for education. Pestalozzi says the following in his *Natural Schoolmaster*:

> It is a great human power to be patient, to wait, until everything matures.

The teacher, to mention another example, now becomes aware quite differently than before, of the threefold aspect of the self referred to by Troxler. He becomes aware of it in the forces of willing, feeling and thinking. Can you educate the will without knowing what it is all about? Of course not, and yet official pedagogical works are almost totally unaware of the forces of the will. The current demand that the will and feeling forces of the child be educated will be futile unless it can stimulate the search for a new knowledge of the human soul forces. Renewing the cultural life of mankind depends largely on whether education succeeds in reaching and strengthening these two forces in the children. That physical education and proficiency in sports cannot achieve this need hardly be mentioned. Anthroposophy as psychology can be the guide to these hidden forces.

We have spoken so much about freedom here that some, to whom authority is not a dirty word, could become uneasy. *How* are children educated, so that they can make *the right* use of their freedom as adults? is not only a justified, but also a crucial question. A superficial and hasty answer would probably be, Only by accustoming children to freedom as soon as possible, by letting them make judgments and decisions at an early age, by bringing them up to be leaders, and by keeping anything that could smack of authority far away from them. Whoever believes this knows nothing of the spiritual laws governing the internal transformations in children, and has no real psychology. His belief is as false as the one which states that the earlier a child's thinking powers are trained, the better they will serve him later. In fact, the reverse is true. There is no better way to smother them.

An individual will be able to make the right use of freedom later, if as a child, and in the most natural way, he is allowed to place himself under the absolute authority of a well-liked adult, if he is able to feel respect for an adult. The respect of a child for a particular person—which is actually respect for the *truth* the way it is silently expressed by that particular adult—is later transformed into respect for the objective truth, independent of any one human being. Thus respect for adults becomes the knowledge and love of truth. As the greatest fruit of knowledge, love wants to act, not theorize. A man who feels this respect for truth knows how to make the right use of the freedom that has been given to him. It is precisely one of these truths that without authority there is no freedom.

Anthroposophy allows an individual to feel such truths, which are so important in education, down to his toes, and that is only one example out of many.

The educational system today can no longer be concerned with the new devices constantly being built by and for experimental psychology. Education is helped only when the teacher is shown how he can develop new organs of perception. With them he can do more than ascertain the current state of "how things are." He can follow the living processes in a child with at least some idea of what is going on. Anthroposophy as psychology is a path to that goal.

When anthroposophy, on the other hand, turns to the world as a whole, it becomes true world-knowledge. No one needs that more than the teacher—the mediator between the child and the world. On him depends whether or not a child awakens to the world in the right way. But first the teacher himself must awaken to this world. He must sharpen and broaden his consciousness, so that he sees in all the world's phenomena, even in the jagged edge of a leaf, the creative and formative activity of the divine spiritual will. If he then brings this world to life for the child, he no longer has dead subject matter in his hands, but something very different. Subject matter, which is no more than matter, kills the living forces in a child. If, however, through the inner power of the teacher who has schooled himself for it, the subject matter still contains what we will call "active ingredients," then each subject will disclose its real and inherent significance as a specific strengthener for the child's soul and spirit. The factual knowledge that results from this process is an additional bonus.

Rudolf Steiner once said: "*The child longs to grasp the divine in nature and in the history of mankind.*" Experience confirms these words a thousandfold. It is just as certain that no child longs for a dogma, for a religious denomination, for a political or other kind of program; he longs neither for pacifism nor nationalism. What he does want is to grasp the spiritual influences on nature and on world history, for they are food for his soul. Rudolf Steiner disclosed the importance of the subject matter when he said that it must act as a medicine in the hand of the teacher. That shows us just how far we still have to go to achieve true education. Or is someone bold enough to claim that he can meet this challenge?

Goethe can act as our guide part of the way, particularly with his "metamorphosis of plants" and his "theory of color." They can become significant because they school

perception and thought in the right way. They are meaningful as methods, however, and not as systems. Goethe did
not consider it important to arrange and classify things neatly and properly. It was the metamorphosis which was important, in other words, the transition from one form of
nature to another. For this a living, active thinking must
first be developed. For Goethe, formulating theories was
secondary to perceiving the original phenomena. That is
possible, however, only through a proper schooling of the
faculties of perception. It is wrong to believe that these faculties of perception are being educated in today's schools.
What follows is a small example out of the science of optics:
In many basic physics textbooks we find the bold statement,
"The beam of white light is refracted by the prism into seven
colors." That is presented to the student as though engraved
in stone, when in fact it is one of Newton's theories, which
even he had to admit was not yet conclusively proven. Newton's color theory is the classic example of a scientific Weltanschauung, and it is now taught to children without a second
thought. Goethe took quite a different approach. With his
heightened faculties of perception and with the help of experiments, he was able to perceive the original phenomena:
those manifestations which, because they have been reduced
to the simplest elements, express their essence the most
clearly. The original phenomenon of light, however, speaks
a completely different language from that of Newton's
theory. The teacher schooled in Goethe will no longer introduce optics by presenting his students with a theory. Instead,
he will lead them slowly back to the original phenomena, so
that these themselves will express their essence, and thereby
the essence of light, to the child. Now, imagine a healthy
child, still very engrossed with color, reading the following
sentence in a physics textbook: Red and green make white,
just as blue and orange or yellow and purple make white.

When such a child reads these theories, he will be greatly amazed and will call out excitedly: "But that's not true at all! When you mix those colors together you end up with a muddy color, not white."

What I have just related is no hypothesis, but a very personal classroom experience.

It is a fact that every theory bars the way to a true knowledge of nature and the spiritual world. Anthroposophy, however, takes Goethe's method of approaching the world's phenomena one step further. It is therefore a path to true world-knowledge. Troxler already said a century and a half ago "*Anthroposophy is the breath and heartbeat of science.*"

Education has only *one* goal, and that is true human education. That is what a teacher should strive for, even if he is reminded of his shortcomings every inch of the way. With this goal before his eyes, he knows himself at one with all great educators and all great figures. He feels the spiritual continuity, in which he himself is permitted to live. He knows he is at one with Troxler, who said: "There is more at stake in education than mere earthly life and civil existence. It is mankind, whose destiny embraces heaven and earth." He knows he is at one with Pestalozzi, and he feels the responsibility embodied in the following words:

> Man is man first, citizen second, and the education of mankind must find its purpose in itself.

The one goal of every educational institution can only be to become an institution for the cultural shaping of mankind. That is true patriotism. "*The reason is clear,*" says Pestalozzi. "*We have spelling schools, writing schools, catechism (Heidelberger) schools only, and we want—men's schools.*"[2] His entire life's work was dedicated to the founding of such a school. Troxler called his unique free school in Arrau, Switzerland, the "educational association," and the "*attempt at a school for humanity.*"

Are such thoughts and efforts anachronistic today? Can timeless truth be oriented according to the prevailing economic situation? Can the teacher act in any way other than *against the dominant influences*? Is he not concerned with the *future*, the way it is being announced in the child? Must he not ally himself with this developing force, which wants to express itself outwardly, in the distant future? Is he the preserver of what is, or the guardian of what is to come?

In the annual report of an educational establishment I recently read the following: "Of particular importance for a school is the method of advancement through the grades." Ought that really to be the case? Of course not. The only important thing in a school is the teacher. Someone who has made it his personal responsibility to develop the proper spiritual present. Everything else, precise rules of advancement, large school buildings, sturdy school desks and black boards, etc., has at the very most only secondary importance. It is the *teacher* alone, a very concrete individual, who ensures that the children are educated and not merely instructed. This responsibility is assumed as an act of free will. It cannot be commanded. This final and absolutely decisive responsibility cannot be taken away from the teacher by any institution, higher authority, organization, lesson plan or regulation. When it comes to making decisions only insightful action, not regulated action is in order. Should the teacher choose not to develop pedagogical insights out of his free human spirit (and no one in the world could force him to), then his mechanical teaching contributes to the barbarity that will surely follow. On the other hand, if as a result of free decisions, he at least tries to become a teacher and therapist, then no matter how modestly he helps the children he contributes to the foundation of a new culture.

Teaching Writing

The writing of adults, as a more or less mechanical skill, is a purely intellectual activity, or an activity of the brain. We have Rudolf Steiner to thank for this fundamental insight, with all its pedagogical and methodological impact.

The intellect is a fairly new human faculty that man acquired only in the most recent stage of his development. To see this still immature human force at work we need only consider all our *technological* achievements. Or we can stroll past a row of houses built, let's say, at the beginning of the century; they, too, are an expression of the intellect. Its most typical expression, however, is the 26 letters of our alphabet. This is why they have become *abstract, conventional* symbols, devoid of life.

They mark the end of a long development, and we may therefore well ask ourselves what stood at the beginning. The answer? Not letters as we know them today—but *pictures*! The writing of the ancient Egyptians or the Mexican Aztecs was a pictography; it is the expression of their inner participation in the world, just as our alphabet expresses present-day man's attitude toward the world. Two different worlds confront us here. Imagine the ancient Egyptian, as out of his imaginative perception he carved his pictures in the stone with hammer and chisel. That kind of writing was still an art which engrossed the *entire* man. Today writing is a function of the head—a mere skill accomplished by three fingertips of one hand. In fact, the slim writing utensil is constantly in danger of slipping out of the fingers altogether.

This distance between writing and the human body would signify the last degree of abstraction.

The first race of people to abandon pictographic writing and to replace it with the game of arranging 26 letters was a race which was already firmly implanted in the physical world: the Phoenicians. The Phoenician alphabet came to us via Greece and Rome, always changing its form according to local conventions.

As teacher of a first grade you are given the task of making these letters approachable for the child.

Close observation reveals that in the seven-year-old child, who is, after all, at the beginning of his earthly development, quite different forces are at work than in the adult. The six- and seven-year-old child, for instance, is closer to the Egyptian in his spiritual makeup, than he is to today's adult. He does not yet possess the forces of the intellect, but has a strong pictorial perception instead; in a way he still has an imaginative consciousness comparable to older human stages of development. That is why the child lives in the world of allegories, symbols, and fairy tales. If we do not wish to harm the child, then we must not present the lesson material in an intellectual form.

More intimate observation of the child as his permanent teeth grow in reveals that he still uses his body much more intensively than he does in later years. He uses his arms and legs, his entire body as a manifold means of expressing his soul's condition. Conversely, however, the child's limbs are an organ of cognition which help him understand many things that an adult understands with his head.

The first grade teacher may now ask himself: How do I present these 26 abstractions, these dead, dry letters, to a child who is very much alive, who still lives so strongly in the imaginative element and in the gesture? For the child, much depends on how this problem in education and methodology is solved. If we want to teach in accordance with the child's being, we must not suddenly introduce that child to the bare bones that are our letters. Instead, we must return to the living *picture*, which only later, after a long development, has become a mere *symbol*. Thus, the activity in the first writing class can properly be only an artistic one. For this reason the children in first grade are taught painting, drawing and clay modeling during their first three months in a Rudolf Steiner School. Painting envelops the child in an ensouled atmosphere and allows him to use his soul forces. Painting speaks to his being, and is the proper introduction to formal lessons in writing. The teacher's task is then to ease this inner artistic activity slowly and carefully into the realm of the intellect, that is, to lead the child gradually from painting to writing.

You may also ask yourself whether it is even possible in a writing class to accommodate the ever fidgeting being that so desperately wants to express itself with gestures, and that experiences life through these gestures. This question brings us to the teacher's *preparation* for the writing class. It is quite an intimate matter and yet is must be discussed. This preparation, unlike that for higher grades, cannot be quantitative, nor can it go into very great detail. It is an inner, *qualitative* preparation.

Above all, we must become aware that we are presenting the children not only with *letters*, but also with what stands behind the letters, namely the *sounds*. If the teacher lovingly lives in the sounds, they will not only reveal their essence to him, but will also tell him *how* he should bring the letters to the children.

By living in the sounds in this way you first become aware of the difference between vowel and consonant. The vowels echo the *soul process* in man. The various shades of feeling of which man is capable live in the vowels. The consonants, on the other hand, can be experienced as imitations of what is happening in the *outside* world.

Part of the teacher's preparation is to feel his way into the essence of each vowel in order to experience its feeling content. What can be experienced in the *Ah*-sound (letter *A*), for example?

It contains the feeling of *amazement*. When we are completely spellbound by something beautiful we live in the *Ah*-mood, and out of the *Ah*-sound stream our soul forces. Imagine the child staring up at the Christmas tree and the way in which the *Ah*-sound flows naturally out of his little soul.

The greatest contrast to the *Ah*-sound is the *Ooh*-sound (letter *U*), the vowel of *fear*. When we are afraid, we withdraw tightly into ourselves; we are at the height of alertness. The mouth is nearly closed, and the *Ooh*-sound is forced out through a narrow opening. All the other vowels lie between these two poles. Out of the *Oh*-sound (letter *O*) speaks purest *sympathy*, a loving embrace. In the *Eee*-sound (letter *I*) we experience something extremely *active*, a strong self-awareness that wants to stride forward in order to conquer the whole world. It is very significant that it is the *Eee*-sound which is heard in the word "me." When the power of "me" combines with the power of love, it can indeed "conquer" the whole world. The *Eh*-sound (letter *E*, as in red), on the other hand, corresponds most to present-day man. It seems to say "Keep your distance! Leave me alone!"

The vowels reveal such feeling content to anyone who makes the effort to penetrate their essence.

The vowels, however, show us something more. They show us how each one corresponds to a visible *gesture*. This fact is like a "secret law of nature." The most beautiful manifestation of this secret law is *eurythmy*. It gives us the gestures which bring the sounds to life in their ideal form. We can also observe these gestures, more or less perfected, in the unspoiled child, and occasionally even in the adult. The Italians are a people who until recently still lived strongly in the gesture, a fact which one of my own experiences may serve to illustrate.

Many years ago I was hiking in the Apennines for a few days with an Italian priest. This man, who in a beautiful and delightful way had managed to retain a certain childlike enthusiasm, was now experiencing the mountains for the first time. On the second day we climbed Mount Cimone, which proved to be quite tiring work. We were soon walking in fog. When we reached the summit of the mountain, however, the blue Italian sky arched over our heads, and a sea of fog was spread at our feet in majestic quiet. The priest was deeply moved by this beautiful sight. He stepped onto an outcropping rock and, in his black soutane, he extended his arms in a perfect *Ah*-gesture and sang a *Te Deum laudamus*. It would be difficult for me to say what made a deeper impression, the magnificence of nature or the profoundly stirred little man in black with outstretched arms.

In the *Oh*-mood the arms or fingers curve, as though wanting to cradle in sympathy what lies before them. Even the mouth forms an oval when it pronounces the letter *O*.

The *Eee*-gesture is a very impressive gesture—active forward striding with arms swinging powerfully forward. It is also, among other things, the gesture which children use in school when a light dawns on them, that is, when they know the answer to a question. They stretch their arm straight up in the air and yell me-e-e-e! This *Eee*-gesture no longer works the same direct way in today's schools, because as a teacher you are virtually forced to make this gesture compulsory for children when they want to speak.

The *Eh*-mood, along with the *Eh*-gesture, is least natural for the child. He does not yet build a wall between himself and others and say: keep your distance! The child knows feelings of admiration, love, joyful excitement, and fear, but he less often feels the urge to ward people off. Adults, on the other hand, put the *Eh*-gesture to good use. How often do you see adults with arms folded across the chest or, particularly in the case of teachers, with hands crossed behind their back? Both are typical *Eh*-gestures.

These gestures, which go with the individual vowels, can bridge the gap between the child and the letters. Rudolf Steiner clearly pointed out one such bridge, going so far as to spell out individual basic instructions. How the writing class takes shape based on these instructions, however, depends both on the children whom destiny has brought together in one class, and on the personality of the individual teacher. If, therefore, I describe in detail how a particular teacher, with a very specific group of individual children, has tried to structure the writing class, that does not mean that some kind of generally applicable norm can be established and used by anyone, any time, and any place. Such imitation would profoundly harm the true pedagogical principle. Merely as a stimulus, however, such examples do serve a purpose. They are passed on for this reason, but in a very personal, completely nonbinding form, as the subject demands.

In order to make the children more conscious of the mood and gesture underlying the individual vowel, I told them the following story when first teaching them "writing": In the olden days there were people who could not speak. When they saw something beautiful, for instance the sunrise, they could not even say Ah! And when they walked past a beautiful rose, they remained mute and did not say: Oh, what a beautiful rose! And when it became dark, and they were lost in the woods and the bad hoot-owl came, they were certainly afraid, but they could not express their fear by saying: Ooh, I'm afraid.—I went on to tell them how angels came down to earth on a rainbow from heaven in order to give men the power of speech. Each wore a robe of a different color and each had a different gesture. The angel who brought the Ah to earth wore a blue robe and stretched his arms wide.—In this way I described how each angel was different in his own special way.

Next I tried to develop the letters out of the gestures. I first created the mood of a certain vowel by telling, or by stimulating the children to tell, a story. In his way they were soon acting out the letters quite on their own.

We climbed a high mountain, saw the river and the lake at our feet, stretched our arms downwards and said Ah!— We knelt down by a flower we loved, enclosed it very gently with our arms and hands and said Oh!—We accompanied a girl who had lost her way in a magic forest and shared all her fears, especially as the big hoot-owl came swooping out of the tree. We reached our arms up over our heads to ward it off and called out Ooh!—The *Eh*- and *Eee*-sounds were also discovered in this way out of the natural mood and gesture. The letter for *Eee* (*I*) unexpectedly became a lit candle, because we always say me-me-me when a little light comes on in our heads.

"Writing" was really painting for many weeks still. For example, the children painted with water colors and broad paintbrushes the angels who had brought the vowels to man. They painted themselves or the figures, the "women," with the various gestures. In fact, they painted everything which had been presented to them in picture form. They also cut angels and people out of colored paper. In this way the children lived in an artistic, ensouled atmosphere for a long time before they had to write the letters in their dead, inartistic form. I let the children take the step from the game of gestures to the abstract by telling them something along these lines: "Look at how you painted the angel who brought the *Ah*, or the "woman" who is saying Ah! with her arms stretched down at her sides. Now, when grown-ups want to write the letter for *Ah* (*A*), they do not paint the whole "woman" or angel. As a matter of fact, many grown-ups have forgotten that the angels brought speech to earth in the first place. They no longer have as much time as you have here in school, and are always in a bit of a hurry. Therefore, they make things much easier on themselves by drawing only the arms and a straight line, like this: *A*! So from now on we want to write the *A* as the grown-ups do." With this the step was taken from the concrete to the abstract. It was linked to a "promise" by the children to paint in the angel's wings at least mentally every time they wrote an *A*.

But even after we had abstracted the conventional letter out of the gesture, we still spent quite a bit of time in the painting atmosphere so suited to the child's being. The letters, too, were first painted with water colors against a colorful background. Only later were they drawn with colored pencils, and lastly written in lead pencil. In that way the long path, which so to speak led from heaven to earth, was covered. As I wrote the alphabet on the blackboard in white chalk for the first time, after the beauty of living color, I could not help but feel sad, even horrified, as I saw the white skeletons of letters. On what kind of a downhill path have you led the children?! You truly are quite a derelict, I said to myself. And to the children I said (silently, of course): I actually feel terribly sorry for you poor little things for being forced to write these letters like this, but that is how grown-ups write. But the children soon cured me of these thoroughly unhealthy feelings. What do you think they did when they saw the slanted, bony letters on the blackboard? They began to laugh boisterously, for such writing seemed exceedingly funny to them. Their laughter said: What strange people grown-ups are. But still, it's so much fun to imitate them and write that way, too. And so they began to write amidst great hilarity and as a kind of game. This experience revealed two truths to me. First, that anything intellectual initially seems comical to children, especially the intellectual adult. And second, that although it is the teacher's job to bring the child down to *earth*, he must do it in the proper way, so that the spiritual origin of things is not forgotten.

Now compare what I have said up to now about the vowels with the pen and ink drawings on Plate 1. I copied them, as well as the later drawings on Plate 2, primarily from the children's pictures. (The beautiful colors of the "originals" have, of course, been lost.)

The little pictures serve to show how the vowels can be developed out of the gestures.

★ ★ ★

A different path altogether leads to the consonants, for their essence is different from that of the vowels. If we would just let ourselves, we could experience them as reflections of outer realities and events. They do not echo man's inner being, but mirror man's entire *environment* through a myriad of pictures. We latch on to this picture-nature of consonants and let consonant-writing become picture-writing, not out of sympathy for the old Egyptians or Aztecs, but because the essence of consonants demands it. Rudolf Steiner's classic example can be mentioned here. In his lectures about the writing class he always cited (among others) the example of the *fish*. He would say something like this: "We draw a fish on the blackboard and talk with the children about fish and about the picture on the board. Then we might say to the children, Now try not saying the whole word fish, but only the very beginning, the *F*. The way you have just said only the beginning of the whole word fish (only *F*) is what

grown-ups do when they want to write that *F*. They also do not write down the whole word fish, but only the beginning, they just hint at it.''—(See plate 2 with the three fishes.)— Rudolf Steiner shed light on an important *methodological principle* with this unassuming example, and as we shall see, it showed me how to proceed.

I told the children the Grimm's fairy tale ''*The Twin Brothers.*'' One of the brothers, with the help of his five animals, the hare, the fox, the wolf, the bear and the lion, succeeds in killing the dragon on Dragon Mountain and in rescuing the King's daughter. But he is betrayed by the King's sly Marshall and sadly takes his leave. One year later he returns to the King's city and sends one animal after another into the King's palace to fetch something to eat from the King's daughter, who is thus being put to the test. The innocent little hare must go in first and it thinks, What am I to do? The dogs in the street will want to tear my beautiful fur! And sure enough, the dogs soon give chase. The poor creature runs zigzag through the streets, causing the dogs to constantly tumble over one another . . .

The children were then allowed to draw a few situations out of this story. First of all, (they would have it no other way) the fight with the dragon, but then the hare which had to zigzag. The dragon, which coils its tail and breathes fire, became the *D* when his evil life was taken. The hare, too, had to give up its life. Only the ears and front paws remained as hare fragments, and became an *H*, and the course the hare had traced on the ground was, of course, made up of lots of *Z*'s.

The principle is always the same: The starting point is the life-carrying picture. Then this life is slowly extinguished, becoming steadily paler, until only the bonelike remains are left—the letter, the way it is used today. (See Plate 2.)

Another example: The children painted the wild ocean

37

with its towering waves and the vulture that flew above them. The waves became the *W* and the vulture the *V*. When the storm has abated, a ship sails over the water. The wind blows merrily in the full canvas, and the fish dare to swim to the surface again and stare astonished at the passing ship. The canvas and the fish present us with two new letters, the *C* and the *F*.

Once I told the story of a brave king who had to fight a troll in order to save this city. The King relied on his trusty sword, and the troll on his strength and the large rock he carried in his hand. After the appropriate speeches and counterspeeches have been made on both sides, the unequal fight begins. The children were allowed to draw these fighting scenes after I, for good reasons, had drawn the two characters on the blackboard for them. (The king's actual task was by no means to fell the troll, but to represent a good, sturdy *K*. As for the troll, unlike the children I did not care much whether he won or lost. His intended role was to represent an impressive *T*.)

The little lights carried by the dwarves in Snow White gave us the shape of the *L*. A nasty snake was made harmless by being turned into an *S*.

There is, especially in northern Germany, a household spirit named Puck. Often he is a hunchbacked little man, and he is a somewhat sensitive being. When his feelings are hurt, which happens easily, he grabs a walking stick and leaves the home. Since he likes children so much, Puck was nice enough to demonstrate a letter for us. When he stands there with his hunchback he looks just like a *P*.

The children particularly liked the story of the gnome. Each night he slipped out of the earth to look at the silvery moon and the twinkling stars. But the closer it came to morning, the sadder he became, because he would have to crawl back into the earth without seeing the sun. So he sat for a few more minutes on his rock, very sad and hunched over. We drew him in this position, with the moon and stars over his head. Later this gnome became the *G*.

In this way every letter could be derived from a picture by later blotting out the picture and leaving the mere abstraction; but for that an entire year would barely suffice. Thus, it is necessary to convey some letters to the children, perhaps those less frequently used such as *X, Q*, etc., in a more direct way. You could, perhaps, write a word or a whole sentence on the board and let the children find and try to guess the still strange letters themselves. That would then be a more analytical process.

An important day for the children is the one on which the teacher writes their names on the blackboard for the first time. On this occasion it is powerfully impressed to the letters. What for us adults is merely a symbol, for children has a life and being of its own. They accept the sounds and letters in their own names in all their reality, and in a way as their destiny. "I have four *A*'s in my name," said one little girl happily. "Oooh, Melissa has two nasty old snakes in her name," a boy yelled out a little tactlessly. "She also has a light and an angel in her name," I said. "That more than makes up for the two snakes!" Now Melissa liked her name all the more. Dallas also had the unlucky snake in his name, but he said to me: "The snake and the dragon (*D*) in front want to blow out the lights in the middle, but the two angels won't let them, right?"

Next I wrote all the letters giant-sized on the floor, and I let the children walk the lines. Where possible, I let them represent the letters themselves. They became, for example, the king, the troll, the gnome. I wished them to experience the form of the letters with their entire body, which is still both a major means of expression and organ of cognition for the seven-year-old child.

Experience has shown that a writing class structured in this way gives the children great joy, for it speaks to their childlike being; and the joy which the teacher himself receives from it, since he is at least modestly creative, is communicated to the children in invisible ways. It would nonetheless be a serious mistake to believe that such a class does not still present the teacher with the greatest difficulties. If I wanted to write about these difficulties, I would also have to speak of many failures and disappointments, all of which have their origin in my own personal inadequacies.

Becoming a teacher means following a long, arduous path leading to a still very distant goal. Countless milestones along this path mark the clumsy moves of which we have been guilty.

I did not want to write about the teacher's path of cognition, however, but about the writing class as a problem of *methodology*. I have attempted to provide an answer to the question, How do I bring the abstract letter forms, this lifeless material, to the child gifted with imagination and a love of gesture without hurting the child's life forces? We find the correct answer in the sounds, if our ears are tuned finely enough to hear them. The vowels tell us: Present us as visible *gestures*, they are the child's bridge to the letters. The consonants, on the other hand, say: Present us as *pictures*, that way the children can pick the letters out of us.

Teaching Arithmetic

Once the teacher begins to think about the nature of arithmetic, the arithmetic class which he must teach presents him with the greatest difficulties. The difficulties come from inside him, and the structure of the class depends on whether the teacher can solve them in his soul (i.e. see through them).

If you open your mind, you can experience arithmetic first as an exclusively human ability that raises him who possesses it far above the animal. The ability to do arithmetic thus becomes an expression of today's *I*-endowed man. Consider how man plunges with his *I* into all seven arithmetic functions (which he himself created), experiencing himself in a new way through each one. Arithmetic allows the *I* to show itself in its manysidedness and power. Yes, there is something wonderful about arithmetic.

But now the other side of the coin: Who among us has not occasionally shuddered when faced with the calculating activity of man, with the calculating man himself? Does that not contradict what I have just said?

This apparent contradiction vanishes when we learn to distinguish between the human force at work in calculating, and the modern application of this psychic force. We may well ask ourselves what purpose such a powerful ability serves for present-day man. Above all, he has learned to turn it into capital, or more precisely, to capitalize on it. He has put arithmetic at the service of egotism, and this much more conspicuously than any other ability. *I* is the name of the creative power active in arithmetic. The exploiter, however, the profiteer, is the "ego." We all know what is meant when we say of a person, "His every move is calculated," and we never completely trust a person considered calculating.

But man is a calculating being in yet another sense and, though it be ourselves, he makes us shudder. We must recognize how man faces the entire universe almost exclusively as a calculating being. Instead of seeking for true understanding, we force all phenomena between heaven and earth into rigid formulas and figures. Nothing is left in our environment that could not be captured in numbers. But part of ourselves (let's call it the heart) resists such calculating activity. It knows that life cannot be grasped with formulas and equations, that it will escape that confinement a thousand times. Experiencing things quite differently, the heart is free to sense the living essence of all things, and resists above all the notion that necessity rules everywhere and freedom nowhere. After all, what message do we receive from calculations? Hard, unyielding necessity! Celestial phenomena are governed by unchanging laws, which can be expressed in formulas. Geologists calculate the age of the earth. In fact, they do even more: They calculate its life span and ignominious demise. Though all these calculations are correct, our heart can still not accept them.

The following story is another small example of how the tendency to approach reality through calculation can become absurd. A movie studio, planning to film the life of Jesus, faces the dilemma of what he looked like. A flyer informs us that rather than using one particular picture of Jesus as a model, his appearance was calculated. We read: "Naturally, this problem (of appearance) was solved analytically by the law of large numbers. We gathered 199 paintings of Jesus by the world's most famous artists, and established their numeric distribution as precisely as possible. Then we traced the various faces on top of one another, making the features common to all of them clearly recognizable.'' That the movie studio's calculations are "correct" is beyond doubt. But more than with other calculations we must wonder whether reality was truly served. Our first uneasiness about the counting and calculating man proves to be well-founded. Richard Wagner added one more to the list of voracious predators: the calculating predator, also known as man.

Here begin the difficulties faced by the thinking teacher. He must wonder whether there is a moral purpose in teaching children arithmetic, since it seems to train them to become calculating predators and profiteers. He will resolve this predicament only when he recognizes that the human force manifested in arithmetic is also the force which makes man human by raising him far above the animal; and when he realizes that if this *I*-power grasps arithmetic in the *right* way, it need no longer turn man into a voracious predator and egotist.

The teacher who has come to this understanding will also no longer be able to accept usefulness as the dominating principle in his teaching of arithmetic. He will no longer restrict himself to teaching the children how to make as much money as possible and how to protect their interests when they grow up. Instead, he will ask himself what kind of forces he is developing in the child through his teaching; whether he is developing them in the proper, healthy way, or in a wrong and therefore harmful way. This is the only approach which places the arithmetic class, as all other classes, at the service of education. In fact, it becomes an extremely important educational tool at the teacher's disposal. What can be developed in the child by an arithmetic class taught in the proper way? Living thinking, thinking that encompasses the realities of life, thinking that arises out of the experience of freedom.

Since arithmetic conforms to and represents natural

laws, it is an understandable tendency to consider it the most unsuitable subject with which to teach a living thinking that is born out of the elements of freedom. Is not calculating thought prefaced by hard necessity? Everything is unambiguous and definite—thus it is not free. A calculation is either correct or incorrect. $2 + 2 = 4$; there are no two ways about it. The moment that $2 + 2$ could also equal 5 the world would come apart at the seams. Is not the very principle of arithmetic rigid, unyielding necessity, or in other words death? And is not arithmetical thinking, when seen in this light, always dead thinking? Where is there still room for living thinking, for freedom?

And yet you can help the children experience freedom in the first arithmetic class. Rudolf Steiner was the first to point out this possibility, for which teachers and pupils alike owe him a great deal.

I will try to show how the first arithmetic class can be structured once it has been recognized as an educational tool with which to mold living thinking. Since the goal of such a class is different from what is generally accepted and expected, you will have to allow me to deviate from the customary approach to teaching it. Some of you might even feel that everything customary is being turned upside down. This is a misconception, however, for in reality everything that has been upside down until now (without your being aware of it) is being turned right side up again. Since time immemorial the natural, legitimate foundation has been the legs, and not the head.

The first task of the arithmetic class is unquestionably to introduce the child to numbers, since counting is the beginning of all arithmetic. The way in which a child is introduced to the numbers is very important. Are they approached in an abstract way or in a living, concrete way? For the teacher, the basic law of biogenesis must now be decisive. Somewhat modified for this case, it could be stated thus: We let the numbers develop before the child in a manner corresponding to the actual birth of numbers. Then we are forced into making a statement that is paradoxical for today's intellectual consciousness; the largest number is one, and all other numbers, as mere fragments of this one, arose out of it. This as yet undivided, unbroken original one is the primary fact; it stands at the beginning. As this divine unity is separated, broken apart, splintered, the numbers arise as secondary facts. By splitting the one, tearing it into two parts, the number two came into being. At the beginning is the whole, which contains the possibility of being divided and subdivided.

The teacher must awaken the child's consciousness to this fact. What tools can he use to accomplish this?

We could take a stick, for instance, and let the child experience it as a whole, and then break it into 2, 4, 8 pieces. The child then observes that by splitting the big 1, the smaller 2, 4, and 8 arise, and that the pieces become smaller the more the stick is broken. Or, we can hand each child a lump of clay, and with his fingers he can knead out of it first two, then four, then finally eight smaller and smaller balls. He then experiences how numerousness arises out of oneness by means of division.

In this way the children are led to experience how numbers are born out of the one. You should avoid taking the opposite abstract approach, in which the fragments are considered the primary fact, and in which one little piece is always glued to the other. The numbers simply did not arise through addition, but through division.

When you have taught the children to experience the numbers in this manner, you can begin teaching them to count. For the teacher, a new factor now comes into play. We can ask ourselves: With what *sense organ* does man perceive arithmetic? We perceive light, sound, etc., with our sense organs. They allow us to form a relationship with the environment. Physical science speaks of five senses. Spiritual science speaks of twelve: the five of physical science, which lie on the surface, and seven others which lie deeper, are more hidden. Steiner called one of these senses the sense of motion. It gives man the ability to perceive the motion he makes or the state of rest in which he finds himself. It is anchored mainly in the limbs and muscles. According to Steiner, it is with this sense that man perceives arithmetic. Confirmed in practice, this statement proves to be of utmost importance for the teacher.

In a certain sense, the limbs are organs of perception, and they can be put to good use in arithmetic. The teacher is thus on the right track if in introducing the children to counting he allows them to join in, to perceive the process as much as possible with the limbs. The arms and legs should be made to count, but keep the head out of it at first. The arithmetic lesson is literally felt in the children's legs, instead of in their heads.

Out of thousands of possible examples from my own teaching experiences, I will now offer a select few. It is simplest if you allow the children to clap energetically with their hands as they count, whereby the accompanying words are accentuated and rhythmic. If you also allow the children to walk at first while clapping and counting, then almost the entire body is involved in counting along. You can also say to the children: Clap twice, four times, six times or twenty-nine times. Or perhaps you say to three children: "You count (and clap) up to five, you up to ten, and you up to fifteen. Later you will count backwards and pick each other up on the way back." The same thing can be done with walking: All three children start to walk; after the fifth step the first child stops, after the tenth the second child, and after the fifteenth the third child. Then counting backwards one child can pick up the next and take it along. The Eurythmy rods come in very handy for counting. In fact, there are virtually limitless possibilities. The children themselves become quite inventive and give the teacher valuable suggestions. Once you have spent a certain amount of time counting with the children in this way, you might just once want to conduct the following experiment: Tell the children to stand perfectly still, put their hands behind their backs, and count to thirty. Then you will see how difficult the children find such counting; how unnatural it appears because it comes from the head, and not from the limbs. (Of course, also this abstract counting must be practiced later!)

Of special importance to the child is the experience of the numbers one, two, three. There are various ways in which to call up this experience. One is to try to raise the following thought into each child's consciousness: I, myself, am like the one, a whole, indivisible. Why? Because I am a human being. (One individuality = one indivisible whole.) But as part of myself, although I am the one, I find the two and the three. I have two eyes, two ears, two arms, two hands, two feet. (My feet take me where I want to go, my hands are there to help my mother and father.) The child also finds the three to be part of himself: The arm is divided into three parts (upper arm, forearm, hand). Each finger has three parts. The leg contains the three (thigh, calf, foot). Needless to say, none of this is brought to the child's awareness as abstractly as I have to describe it here. In the higher grades you can go one step further and show how the body expresses the numbers internally as well. The lungs, for example, are divided into two's and three's. (One = 2 + 3.)

Once the children have learned the numbers in this fashion and can count a little, we allow them to take a first step toward actual arithmetic. What method must we use if arithmetic is really to become an educational tool for living thinking? Broadly speaking, we must start with living reality, not with abstractions. The reality from which we set out is the *one*, but not an abstract one (which is nothing more than a fragment of the one), but a whole, a unity, which contains all the fragments. In other words, I do not begin with a single apple, then place another one beside it, in order to teach the children the addition $1 + 1 = 2$. I begin instead with a big pile of apples. It is then out of this unity, this one, that arithmetic must commence. You may, of course, use a pile of kidney beans or horse chestnuts as visual aids instead of apples—the principle itself is not changed.

I have, for example, *one* pile of chestnuts on the table around which the children stand (if the class is too large for this, I am confident you will have no trouble coming up with another arrangement). The children quite naturally experience this pile as a whole. It is something very concrete for them, definitely the "primary fact." If you now allow them to count the individual chestnuts they will experience how numerousness lives inside oneness. It is this numerousness which permits us to calculate in the first place. Let us say the one pile contains 12 chestnuts. We let the children "calculate" with it by letting them divide the pile into all kinds of smaller, always different piles. The child finds himself in an element of freedom in the truest sense. Limitless possibilities are open to his consciousness, and he experiences manifoldness and creative freedom as the beginning of arithmetic. On the other hand, if the child is introduced right off the bat to one specific arithmetic operation, usually addition, the first calculation he must experience is $1 + 1 = 2$. He is thus immediately thrust into the realm of necessity. Instead of creative numerousness he must experience unbending compulsion. This will affect him for the rest of his life.

To stay with our example, assume that the child divides

the pile of chestnuts into three smaller piles of 7, 3, and 2. Through this action he learns that 12 is 7 and 3 and 2. By then dividing the pile in a different way, the child learns that the same 12 can also be 4 and 5 and 3, or 8 and 4, or 3 and 2 and 4 and another 3, etc.

It is good to practice this nonrigid "pile arithmetic" as long as possible. The time spent doing so is by no means wasted, for all four arithmetic operations are performed each time the pile is rearranged. It is really true that one "calculation" can be seen as division, multiplication, addition and subtraction. An example: The child divides the single pile of chestnuts (the 1) into 4 smaller equal piles. What is involved in this seemingly insignificant act? First, the splitting of 1 into 4. (Out of the 1 comes the 4!) Second, a division, for it is revealed that the pile (containing 12 chestnuts, the child counted them), divided into 4 parts, produces the 3. (There are 3 chestnuts in each little pile.) Whether verbally expressed or not, the child experiences the calculations: 3 is 12 divided by 4. At the same time he realizes that 12 is 4 times 3 (a multiplication), and 12 is 3 plus 3 plus 3 plus 3 (an addition). You can also let the child see that 3 is 12 minus 9 (a subtraction). All four of these arithmetic operations are visible in that one simple act. But they are not abstract nor rigid. Rather than being sharply separated from one another, one spills over into the next. Herein lies the significance and the teaching aspect of "pile-arithmetic," and for that reason it should be practiced as long as possible.

Later, however, it becomes necessary to separate what lives, so to speak, as living chaos into the four realms of division, multiplication, subtraction and addition. Every operation then becomes a world unto itself. With which world do we begin? The answer is that it is not so important to which operation the child is introduced first. What matters is the way in which that introduction is made. For purely traditional reasons, I will begin my discussion with addition.

In addition we deal with the sum and the two addends. After what has been said about the birth of the numbers out of the one and about "pile-arithmetic," it should be clear that the primary fact, that which represents the true beginning, is the sum, and by no means the parts, the addends. Mentally, the child always grasps the whole first, and only later does he see the individual parts as well; only after he has looked over the whole basket of apples (the pile) does he reach for a particular one. Translated into the language of arithmetic, this means that the child mentally grasps the whole first, and only later does he see the individual parts as well; only after he has looked over the whole basket of apples (the pile) does he reach for a particular one. Translated into the language of arithmetic, this means that the child mentally grasps the sum first and then moves on to the addends. This corresponds to the child's, as yet not intellectual consciousness. It is toward this consciousness that the teacher should orient arithmetic, not toward his own. This is why he does not begin addition with the addends, but with the sum, and lets the child experience, for example, $7 = 3 + 4$, $7 = 2 + 5$, $7 = 4 + 3$. (In visible form, the one pile of 7 chestnuts can be divided into 2 smaller piles of 3 and 4, or 2 and 5, or 4 and 3 chestnuts.) This kind of addition can be called living, for it reflects the many-sidedness of real life. The child becomes aware that life is full of possibilities; his thinking can develop in its original, living way. (The same 7 is not only $3 + 4$, but also $2 + 5$, etc.) Dead addition, however, $(3 + 4 = 7)$ from the outset forces the childish thinking into a straightjacket from which it can never fully extricate itself. On the one hand, limitation, on the other, limitlessness and plenty.

This does not mean, however, that the child should be spared the dead form of addition forever. That would be irresponsible even toward the child, who must later adapt to the civilization created by intellectual man. So when a child has lived in living addition for a while and has schooled his thinking by it, he may and must be introduced to dead addition as well (1 + 1 = 2). At that point, it can no longer hurt him very much.

To illustrate the appropriate path the teacher should take in introducing the children to subtraction, I would like to mention a personal experience. One day a five-year-old friend and I went for a walk in a park. The little tyke was carrying a few peanuts in his hand to feed to the trusting little birds. They came one after the other and made off with the delicious little nuts until finally only three were left. At this point the child said to me: "Hey, I started out with seven nuts, now all I have are three. How many did the birdies fly away with?" This childish question is very informative and indicates the right approach to subtraction. What was the chain of events leading up to the child's question, which is nothing other than a subtraction problem? First, he looked in his hand and noticed the meager remainder of his previous cache. So the first thing is the remainder. Then he remembered the little horde of nuts that he had to start out with. The second thing is thus the sum. What he does not know, however, because it must be calculated, is what was taken away. The arithmetically correct answer to the precocious little inquisitor's question would have to be the following: The three you now have in your hand came to be because from the seven, which you still remember (although you no longer have it), the four was whisked away. You could not have known that it was four nuts, because they are now in the dark little bellies of the sparrows where you cannot see them. The reason I know this, is because I can do arithmetic. Once you go to school you, too, will be allowed to learn arithmetic like the grown-ups.

The most concrete thing for the child is thus the remainder, or the difference. (The sum is much less real in this sense.) The difference should therefore be the starting point of subtraction for the child, at least in the beginning. I have a pile of 9 chestnuts, for instance. I take a few away and ask the children: how many remain on the table? There are five. How many were there in the beginning? Nine. How many did I take away? This subtraction problem translated into figures looks like this: $5 = 9 - ?$ Without somehow getting lost in abstraction I could also set up the problem this way: You see the pile of chestnuts here. Now count how many chestnuts are in it. Nine. But I do not want nine chestnuts, I want five. How many must I take away? This is the process of living subtraction. Naturally, I do not always have to cling to that pile of chestnuts. There are countless other possibilities. The following example should serve not as a blueprint, but merely as a suggestion. The children and I speak of what happens at day's end, when darkness falls, and the stars begin to sparkle in the night sky. Then I draw twelve stars on the blackboard. Along comes a dark cloud and covers all but three of the stars: a yellow one, a red one and a blue one. But how many stars did the big cloud cover?

What applied to addition also applies to subtraction: Once the child's thinking is strengthened by living subtraction (for example, if he has experienced $5 = 7 - 2$, but also $5 = 9 - 4$ or $5 = 8 - 3$), he may and must learn dead subtraction in its rigid necessity ($7 - 2 = 5$).

A few words about multiplication and division: If you immerse yourself in these two worlds and attempt to grasp them in their inner life, you may experience something quite strange. The walls that usually separate them dissolve, and the two worlds begin to mingle to such an extent that in many cases you begin to wonder: Is this a multiplication or a division? Figuratively speaking, the situation resembles that of the soul and spirit forces in the human being: both are worlds in their own right, but one spills over into the other, so that a highly developed inner sight is necessary to differentiate between the two.

In order to demonstrate how closely related multiplication and division are, consider the following arithmetic problem: What number contains the 8 seven times? Is this division or multiplication? It looks like multiplication if I write down as: ? = 8 × 7. The problem will be solved, however, only if it is set up as: ? : 8 = 7, in other words as a division problem, even though it acts like multiplication. In general we can say that when inverted, multiplication becomes division.

Let us also inform ourselves on the methodically correct (i.e. realistic) path toward these two calculations. If we consider the whole, the not yet differentiated, as the reality from which the teacher must develop the lesson, then in multiplication it can only be the product, whose differentiations are the two factors (multiplicand and multiplier). Accordingly, I will let the children first experience, for example, 12 = 3 × 4, 12 = 2 × 6, 12 = 4 × 3, 12 = 6 × 2, in order to show them how various factors can be used to produce one and the same quantity. There are many ways to arrive at one quantity, depending on the angle from which you approach it. Through such arithmetic exercises the child develops a living thinking, whereas abstract multiplication (3 × 4 = 12), weaves such a tight web around thinking that it loses its freedom of movement. This kind of multiplication must therefore not be taught in the beginning, but only after the child has learned to think in the living multiplication.

In division, special emphasis should be placed on the fact that measuring and dividing are two very different arithmetic acts. To illustrate this, consider these two problems:

56 chestnuts = 7 × ? chestnuts
56 chestnuts = ? × 8 chestnuts

In the first problem the multiplicand is missing. The question is: How big is one seventh of 56 chestnuts? We are dealing with the parts here. The second problem, however, is looking for the multiplier. Rather than dividing the 56 chestnuts into seven equal parts, we want to establish how often the small pile of eight chestnuts is contained in the large pile of 56 chestnuts. We are not dividing, we are measuring. Both examples illustrate how closely multiplication and division are related.

The approach to division corresponds to what has already been said. Begin with the quotient (the remainder) and with the sum (example: $5 = 10 : ?$ or $5 = 15 : ?$).

Developing and practicing the multiplication tables is very important in the first arithmetic class. You can start with counting, while at the same time addressing the child's sense of motion. You could, for instance, let the children count together loudly and rhythmically (while clapping their hands) from 1 to 20. Then say to them: Now clap hard for one number, but for every second number just tap your fingertips together; say the number that you clap out loud, say the number that you do not clap very softly, so that I can barely hear it. The children then count: one, *two*, three, *four*, five, *six*, seven, *eight*, etc. This produces the sequence 2, 4, 6, 8, etc., which in the end can be practiced out of the rhythm, purely by memory, before the multiplication table has been developed. For these preliminary exercises experience shows that there is also a myriad of options open to the teacher, so that the children join in every day's activities with new enthusiasm and inspire the teacher with their own ideas.

The multiplication tables are themselves developed out of living multiplication (not out of dead addition!). As an example, I will attempt to present aphoristically how I developed the "two-times table" for the children. We laid the big blackboard on the desk and stood around it. Then I put one pile of brown chestnuts on the blackboard; they were not chestnuts now, but one flock of little white sheep asleep in a stall. (I outlined the walls of the stall with chalk.) The stall had a narrow door just wide enough to allow two sheep to pass through side by side. I asked the children, "How many sheep are in this stall?" (20.) Then I asked, "How often can a pair of sheep go out of the door together? The children must look to see how often two goes into twenty. (How must I divide twenty so that two are always taken away?) The children soon discovered, and I also showed them concretely, that 2 goes into 20 ten times, or 20 is 10 times 2 ($20 = 10 \times 2$). After grazing all day, the sheep wander back into the stall in the evening. During the night the bad wolf comes, slips through a hole in the stall and snatches a pair of sheep. Without letting the children know how many, I take two chestnuts away and say, "Count how many sheep are left." (There are only 18.) "How many did that bad wolf snatch?" (Example of living subtraction: The 18 originated by taking two away from the whole, 20.) So, now we have only 18 sheep left. When the shepherd opens the door in the morning, he will no longer watch ten pairs of sheep pass by him. "What do you think," I ask, "how often can the 18 sheep go out to graze two by two until the stall is empty?" (How many times does 2 go into 18?)—As the wolf, for the teacher's sake, keeps strangling two innocent sheep a night with relentless cruelty, we arrived at the complete two-times table, but in this form:

$$20 = 10 \times 2$$
$$18 = 9 \times 2$$
$$16 = 8 \times 2 \text{ etc.}$$

We began with the highest number, again and again started with the entire pile (which grew steadily smaller) and multiplications (which are actually divisions). The children practiced it first in this form, admittedly purely from memory, but with the intensive participation of the arms and legs, and in rhythms spoken out loud. One day I said, "Okay, without further ado we will now turn the entire two times table upside down!" That struck the children as very funny. ("What strange people grown-ups are.") When the two-times table is upside down it looks like this:

$$1 \times 2 = 2$$
$$2 \times 2 = 4$$
$$3 \times 2 = 6 \text{ etc.}$$

This method of developing the multiplication tables out of living multiplication is naturally only one among many; each teacher will have to structure the class differently when it comes to the details. It would be unfortunate if a reader of this essay were simply to copy the story of the wolf and the sheep.

Steiner has pointed out that it is not good for a child to practice only *one* arithmetic operation for a fairly long period of time, say six months; on the contrary, all four operations should be presented to the child almost simultaneously. To nonrigid thinking this demand will make sense. Man himself does not grow for six months exclusively with his legs, then later (perhaps in the "fall semester") with his arms. Why not? Because man is a living organism in which the individual forces are in true interplay.

Practicing only one kind of arithmetic, however, means forcing the soul forces of the child to grow in one direction only. This is no less unnatural than if it were in the teacher's power to let first the legs of the children grow, and then to "go on" to something else later. Our abstract (upside-down) thinking easily misleads us into such unnaturalness, into such abstractions. This kind of thinking has also turned the first arithmetic class upside down. We must turn it right side up again. If we do this, it rewards us by turning into an invaluable educational tool, which the teacher would never want to give up. Then arithmetic has something beautiful about it.

"Local History" in First and Second Grade

The lesson plan in the Free Waldorf School states the following regarding local history in the first two grades:

> Local history should gradually awaken the dreaming child to his environment so that he learns to associate with it in a more conscious way. The familiar plants, animals, stones, mountains, rivers, and meadows that are brought to the child's awareness and introduced to his understanding must never be described by the teacher in an abstract way. In keeping with the child's stage of life, he must present everything in a way that addresses the child's *fantasy and moral imagination*.

How does this educational principle relate to the well-established methodological principle that states, Proceed from near to far, from familiar to unfamiliar? According to this methodological precept you should begin the lesson with what is closest to the child, moving gradually to more remote things. Like so many other catchwords or phrases, the truth of this precept is beyond doubt—but only as long as it remains an abstraction, a theoretical demand.

It is an entirely different story when you study how some schools carry out this old-fashioned methodology. Then it must be said that its practical application in the school can make the teacher with even the slightest knowledge of children feel rather apprehensive. He might say to himself: But this means standing the entire local history class on its head. How could that have happened? The answer he must give himself is: Because the knowledge of the child's soul, origin and purpose on earth is no longer alive in our culture.

If we are supposed to progress from near to far in local history, then surely the next, very serious question we must ask ourselves is: What is, in fact, closest to the child? Are children similar to adults in this respect, or do completely different conditions and laws apply? Is it not possible that what is close to us adults is worlds away from the child, and that worlds separate us from what is close to the child? The curricula and school procedures provide a ready answer to this question. They tell us that the child is no different from the adult in this respect. What is near and far for one is near and far for the other. The adult feels close to the room in which he sits, the house in which he lives, the town in which he spends his life. It follows that the first local history class must begin with the classroom: Count the four walls and the doors, the windows and chairs; don't forget the waste basket; measure the dimensions of the room and draw a careful and accurate floor plan. The student thereby gains an important mental image: in the beginning was the classroom. This microcosm, this primordial cell then expands into the school building, the school grounds, the town, the district, the county. Bigger and bigger pieces are added until they become so large that local history is shoved aside to make room for geography. Then, toward the end of the child's years in school, geography, in turn, makes a giant and quite unexpected leap into the universe, suddenly appearing before the students' eyes as astronomy. Thus, over many years the children journey from the classroom up to the stars. Those stars, however, have no relationship to the earth.

Faced with this generally accepted journey we once again ask the crucial question: What is close to the seven- and eight-year-old child? What does his world look like? Is it the chair on which he sits, the notebook in which he writes, the playground in which he romps? Or is he perhaps even more deeply connected to the sun, moon and stars? Does not the individual child's soul journey from the stars down to the earth? Is what is close to his body also close to his soul? Or is he closest in his "consciousness," in his "thoughts," precisely to the heavenly bodies, as well as to clouds and wind, trees and flowers, water and fire? Does he not live particularly deeply and vividly with these things as long as he remains unspoiled? And does not the small child find the classroom, the house, the town, everything planned and built by men to be foreign, far removed and incomprehensible? He who has learned how to observe correctly knows this to be true.

When a teacher understands these facts, the consequences are significant. He will no longer begin with the classroom in local history. So, where will he begin? The "point" where he must begin his lesson can then be only one thing: the whole world. In the beginning was the whole world— that is a mental image which is closer to the child than the one mentioned above, which elevates the classroom to the origin of all existence. In the beginning was the universe: the entire earth and the heavenly bodies, the plants they created, nurtured and formed, and of course the animals. Also that which lives between heaven and earth: The wind and the clouds. But also water and fire, and countless other beings. Experience shows that the journey which begins with the entire universe is the right one.

How did the misunderstanding about what the child is close to occur? It occurred because the adult, who, after all, experiences the world in a manner not merely slightly but fundamentally different from the child, has transferred his own Weltanschauung to the child.

It can only benefit the educator if he regularly attempts to clarify in his own mind how he as an adult perceives the world, and how the child experiences it.

Man has a wonderful privilege over other beings: As the

achievement of a long human development, he grasps the world with his reasoning powers, also called the intellect. With this reasoning, however, he grasps only what is lifeless in nature, what is dead. He may be able to examine the body of a living being with his reasoning powers, but he cannot use them to grasp the life-giving force in this body. Some might consider it a sad commentary that in order to understand the nature of a thing we must first kill it, even if only by thinking about it too much. Only that which has been deprived of life can be researched, registered or systematized ("experienced" would already be too strong a word) by the intellect.

The child experiences the world very differently. The more we watch him, the clearer it becomes: The child has no connection to dead things yet, which makes his connection to living things that much stronger. He finds the life in every object and forms a bond with it. Thus, he does not register and systematize yet, but simply experiences in the true sense of the word. It is as if the child wanted to breathe life even into the "dead," like the creator himself. The adult kills where there is life in order to understand. The child finds the life in all beings and even gives life to things which do not seem to be the direct bearers of life.

Why can the child experience the world as filled with live beings? Because quite different soul forces are at work in him than in the adult. The forces of the intellect are still embryonic, still being developed. The child's "forces of cognition" lie deeper. The organ of cognition is not the self-enclosed head, but the living thought body. Although our thinking must be seen as dead in a certain sense, the child's "thinking" may be called alive. Thus, he neither can nor wants to understand the world in concepts, abstractions and definitions as yet, but in living images, which embody more of reality than arid, rigid concepts.

We could almost be tempted into saying that the child

experiences his entire environment with his fantasy, if this much used, devalued expression were not already understood as something abstract, a mere combining ability, instead of a real creative force that penetrates the living reality of things. Watch a five- or six-year-old child; how he lives with his environment; the little thing is forever immersed in his creative activity (unless forcibly dragged out by adults). Like a little God he constantly creates new worlds for himself. The worlds already in existence are all his friends. He speaks to sun and moon, mountain and stream, dog and bird, stone and stick as though to his equals. He is connected to them through forces which are no longer present in the adult, or at least do not appear to be. These are forces for which the adult no longer even has a definite name (although naming things usually gives him such pleasure), so foreign have they become to him, so far back do they lie, so deep are they buried in him—and so close are they nevertheless.

In the unspoiled eight-year-old child these forces are still extraordinarily active. At this age the child must therefore not be abruptly introduced to the dead world of the adult. Doing so would kill the most valuable forces of the child. The fairy tale of the toad, handed down from the time of ancient knowledge, serves as reminder and warning for the teacher. What does the story tell us? There is a little girl, and every day her mother gives her a bowl of bread and milk. (The mother thus takes great care in providing for the physical needs of her child.) The child takes the food and sits in the courtyard with it. Each time she begins to eat, a toad comes along, lowers its head into the milk and eats with her. (The toad can live on dry land as well as in water, two different worlds. Could it not represent a mediator between two worlds, which, though different, still border on one another?) The toad shows its gratitude by fetching the child all sorts of beautiful objects out of the deep, dark cellar as presents from another world: sparkling stones, pearls and golden playthings. The mother provides for the child's physical needs, but the loyal toad ensures that the child's soul never lacks for golden playthings. With this double nourishment the child can thrive and bloom. One day, however, the mother discovers the friendship between the child and the toad. She runs out of the house with a stick and kills the good animal. Although the girl continues to receive plenty of rolls and milk each day, she loses her red cheeks, falls ill, and before long she lies on her deathbed. It is the child's soul that lies there.

Anyone who wants to can understand this story. It is a guide for parents and teachers. The task is to ensure that the child's soul does not die. The child must have a toad to be its mediator between the sense perceptible, visible world and the other world. Out of the fairy tale speaks a "pedagogical demand," one that Rudolf Steiner expressed so often and in so many different ways. This demand, however, is of enormous importance. The teacher, to stay with our image, should not only allow the toad to live, he should himself become the mediator between the external, visible world and the living soul world by fetching the golden playthings for the child so that he can play with them, that is, can nourish his soul from them. This is an awesome task. It presupposes that the teacher has connections to the "other world." But unless he is a born poet, the teacher, according to his age and education, is an intellectual being just like any other adult, closer to the mother with her stick than to the toad. So what must he do? The answer then, which applies not only to the local history class, but also to education as a whole, must ultimately be the following: The teacher must try to awaken forces in himself besides those of the intellect, forces which lie deeper than "superficial" reasoning. We can call them the forces of childhood, for they are natural to the child. The teacher must make what we could call his living thought body more active, so that he can understand the child's soul processes on the one hand, and nature's living processes on the other. This is no longer an ordinary understanding, but rather a pictorial recreating of the living processes in man and nature. Does this mean that the teacher is supposed to become an artist or a poet? Yes and no. Not in the sense that he absolutely must paint and write poems, but in the sense that he understands the natural processes occurring around him, that in him they give rise to images, and that he offer these images to the children in the first local history class, for example, in order to awaken them to their environment and arouse their interest in accordance with their inner possibilities.

This is all much easier said than done for amateurs such as we all still are. What we are dealing with here (it would be hard not to notice) is a path of inner knowledge that the teacher must walk. If the teacher can take this path of inner development, it becomes possible for him to interest the child in the whole environment in an "imaginative and moral way," in other words, to teach a class in local history in a way suited to the child.

What I have just described is the ultimate goal toward which we strive, but which is far from being attained. In fact, we have taken at most a few timid steps in that direction.

The following is a very small, very limited excerpt out of a first local history class the way it once occurred under a particular set of circumstances. It should be considered only as a teacher's experiment, undertaken with extreme caution, in an attempt to go in the direction indicated above. I would never go so far as to proclaim the experiment "a success," but it did confirm many things and therefore gave me courage to continue on the path I had chosen. I am assuming that none of my readers will regard my description as a recipe that can simply be borrowed for his or her own school kitchen. It would no longer produce a tasty dish. The example is one of a kind, but its underlying "idea" has general validity.

I cannot get around prefacing my descriptions with a few personal observations. I have quite a long walk to school every day. I do not walk alone, but with a companion, a seven-year-old girl. Naturally, I must tell her stories along the way. She also asks me lots of questions, about the clouds, whether you could sit on them, whether you could peek into heaven from them, whether the wind is a friend of the clouds, or is mean to them. The path also takes us past beautiful trees: birch trees standing in the garden, a huge linden tree, beech trees, and strong oaks. By the child's questions I notice how intimate a child's relationship to the trees is, and how the trees live as living beings in the child's soul. I wonder to myself, Should I speak with the children about the trees during a local history class? After I say yes to myself, I also know that I must penetrate more deeply into the inner being of trees than before, and that I want to learn to love them even more, particularly the trio of the birch, linden and oak that I can greet every day with my child companion.

I will mention only sketchily the first class hour in which trees became the center of attention. For a long time I had been unsure how I should begin, for it did not seem like a good idea simply to tell the children of my three trees. I decided to ask the children a question, hoping their answer would help me discover how I should proceed. What I asked was approximately this: "When you walk to school each day you pass by many trees. But tell me, do you like the trees?" To this the children yelled, "Yes, yes." One of them called out, "I know a beautiful poem about trees." "Oh, me, too," and "me, too," yelled a second and a third. "Would you like to recite it?'' I asked. They started right in, first just the three of them, but soon the others joined in quietly, and already the second time around the entire chorus chimed in with noisy enthusiasm. It was the poem by Albert Steffen, ''Let us Love the Trees.'' I had actually had that poem ''reserved'' for the end of this main lesson block (see translator's preface), but as I heard the children recite the poem so joyfully, I thought how wonderful it was that the children themselves had found the right beginning.'' Thus I can take no credit for the beginning turning out well.

I then asked the children, ''But is there perhaps one tree that you especially like?'' One child answered, ''I like the weeping willow the best,'' and another said, ''That's the one I like best, too.'' A wild little boy called out, ''I like the pine tree best.'' I was rather amazed by this, and I asked him why he liked the pine tree so much. ''Well,'' he answered, ''you know when the wind blows through the pine tree? It makes such a loud rustling noise, and I really like that.— This answer reassured me. ''And what tree do you like best?'' I asked another child. ''The linden,'' came the response.

Then the children began to take turns telling stories about the trees, sometimes even telling them simultaneously. Each one spoke of his trees as if of good friends. The essence of the children's being as well as that of the trees became more and more clear to me. I then sketched a birch tree on the blackboard and said, among other things, ''You know, it has such long arms and merry hands. It can never be still. When a child passes by the birch waves at him, moving its arms and fluttering its hands like this.'' (I demonstrated.) Promptly a child fluttered out of her seat, hopped around the classroom and called, ''I am the birch tree. This is how it says hello, waves and greets the children.''—I had a tough time getting the child to sit down again.

After the birch tree I drew the oak. Solidly it stood there

and braved the storm with powerful arms.—At this point the wild little boy came to me, gripped my arm and said, "You know, I like the pine tree because it rustles, but I like the oak tree even better."

Once I had collected my thoughts after this first class, I tried to think over what I had been shown. I said to myself, The children love the trees as their good companions. But each child has one with which it shares a special friendship. It is as if that particular tree would incorporate the child's own characteristics or special temperament. Have not the melancholic children chosen the weeping willow as their favorite? And the boy who so enjoys dreaming undisturbed about his existence, who loves comfort and prizes coziness above all else, this little phlegmatic, has he not singled out the linden tree as his friend? And the other boy with the kind, but so often quick-tempered, irascible, and choleric disposition, who becomes intoxicated with the rustling of the pine trees, how quickly he became enamored of the defiant oak tree and chose it as his leader. And the little girl with the curls who could not sit still the whole year because she has a butterfly nature, the little sanguine, how she began to dance lightly and flutter her hands as the slender, light birch tree came to life before her eyes. I told myself that I would have to build the rest of my lesson upon these inner relationships in an "imaginative and moral way." Okay then, I will give each child the tree that he needs for his particular temperament. The tree shall live, speak and act before the child's eyes in all its beauty, but also in its uniqueness and one-sidedness. The child should experience the tree as the mirror-image of his own nature.

Of course, it is impossible to repeat here what transpired in each individual class, nor was I the only one to tell stories. It was rather a mutual feeling by the children and myself. My personal task was primarily to ensure that the thread of the "story" did not get lost. Often it was a question and answer period. In any case, things did not fall into place as neatly as I will try to summarize here.

Once upon a time there was a big garden in which grew beautiful flowers and many trees. A weeping willow, a birch, an oak and a linden tree were also there, and fairly close to one another so that they could still speak together easily. As different as they were, it almost seemed as though they belonged together.

The *weeping willow* stood apart the most. She likes standing apart. She speaks little. She stands there alone, arms hanging low. She is always a little sad, and frequently complains about the evil world. She loves the gray winter days; when they come she is apt to say, "Look at these days without color and without shine. They are honest, they show how the world really is, yes, that is what the world looks like."—She likes rainy weather, too. She likes it when the sky hangs heavy with clouds. The raindrops fall on the weeping willow and she says, "Those are my tears, which I am shedding. I must cry, because so many sad things happen in the world." How happy the weeping willow is, however, when night falls. She greets every little star in the sky, not boisterously, but quietly and with great warmth. The little stars in the sky return the greeting and say to one another, "We will give this silent, lonely tree our special love." The moon, too, is a good friend of the willow. It casts down a silver dress, almost too beautiful and bright for words. That makes the sad willow feel better. How could she not love the moon now?—But when the sun shines, the birds sing, and the wild children shout with joy and somersault around her, then she feels very uncomfortable, because she can no longer feel as sad as she would like. For she enjoys being somewhat sad and pensive all the time.

Farthest away from the weeping willow stood the *birch*

tree. She wears a light, airy dress. Unable to hold still, she loves to dance, especially in the spring. She greets everyone, waves to them from a distance and calls, "Hello, how are you?" She is always merry and she loves the whole world, the sun and the clouds, the beetles and the summer birds. When a bird flies by, she calls to it, "Sit down by me and sing me a song, I so love to be entertained. I cannot tell you how much boredom frightens me." The little bird comes and sings a song, and the birch laughs, "Oh, how beautiful and interesting the world is. You see something new every minute. No, you never have to be bored."—The birch does not like the rain, and after a rain shower she shakes herself in order to dry off as soon as possible. But the sun she loves. She calls up, "Dear mother sun, how nice to see you again. Be so kind as to find out where the frisky wind is hiding and tell him to come out." No sooner said, than along comes the frisky wind and romps through the birch. He takes her in his arms and twirls her about. The birch shouts with joy, "The world cannot be more wonderful than it is right now." She is completely happy and excited. Only at night does the birch settle down. The evening star comes, enfolds the little tree in the arms of its rays, looks at her gently and says, "You are my sweet little earth child." The little birch is blissfully happy and says softly, "Playing with the frisky wind may be fun, but resting in my mother's arms is a thousand times better."

In the middle of the garden is the *linden tree.* Big and broad she stands there. She needs a lot of room. She does not chatter as much as the birch tree, not because she is sad like her other neighbor, the weeping willow. No, she is quiet because she prefers to dream. She feels best basking in the noon heat of the summer months. It is so still then. No one is making any noise, everything sleeps or dreams; even the pesky wind has lain down somewhere and gives no thought to disturbing the good linden tree in her peace and comfort. Thousands of little bees come and go, but that does not bother the linden tree. She says almost in her sleep, "Come to me little bees, my flowers give you honey. I have enough for all of you. I am dripping with sweet honey." It is completely still, only the little bees buzz and buzz. The linden tree dreams, and any human passing by breathes in the flower-scented air, closes his eyes, begins to dream, too, and is full of sweet well-being, just like the linden tree herself.

And there is still the *oak tree*. Solidly he is anchored to the ground. He stretches his powerful arms left and right, up and down. And what fists he makes! Yes, so bold and wild is he that you could almost be frightened of him. It is good that we can say to him, "Listen, oh mighty oak tree, we are your good friends." But then where is the enemy? Is it the bees or the Summer birds? No, no! Nor is it the whistling wind. The oak tree just laughs at him. But autumn brings him, the enemy. It is the storm wind! The oak tree calls, "Hey, you, storm wind, come here and show me how strong you are. You're not afraid of me, are you? But the storm wind is not afraid, he comes raging in, grabs the oak tree by the arms and hair and shakes him until his limbs creak. But the oak is strong and brave. He defends himself and braces against the storm. Long does the battle rage. Now the storm wind has torn an arm off the oak and sent it flying way out into the field. The disaster gives the oak new courage, he fights valiantly. Finally the storm wind tires. He makes peace with the strong oak and goes on his way. Once he is gone the oak tree says, "My, that was wonderful! When he comes back I will do battle with him again. I am already looking forward to next autumn!"

In this way we got to know the four trees together. (Later there would be others.) It was plain to see how each temperament felt drawn to one of these four tree representatives, and really identified with it when it came to its good sides. During the battle between the oak tree and the storm wind the choleric child could give vent to his energy, particularly when he was allowed to portray the oak, call to the storm and engage him in battle. The phlegmatic child closed his own eyes and offered a picture of sweet contentment as we spoke of the linden. The sanguine child could not do enough to imitate the birch every morning. And no one could portray the gloomy or pensive weeping willow better than the melancholic child.

Later I went further still in my characterization and related the trees directly to humans themselves. It went something like this: It came about that the four trees in the garden fell to chatting. Even (what a miracle) the weeping willow and linden tree joined in this time. What were they talking about? About big and little people. Each tree revealed its relationship to them.

The weeping willow says:

I prefer adults to children, because adults are quieter and more reasonable. They do not make so much noise. You see, I really cannot bear noise. Well-behaved and quiet children I do not mind. Such a child comes by here every day; she looks out at the world with serious eyes. Perhaps she has a secret worry. If I could just ask her, how gladly I would help. But I do not dare. I just say to her quietly every day, Yes, you and I, we belong together.

The birch tree says:

No, it is the adults that I do not like. They can no longer really laugh and sing and be merry. Amazing that such things can be forgotten. But children I like. The merrier they are, the better I like it. I call to them, Come over and dance around me. Then the girls and boys come, link hands, hop in a circle around me and shout with joy. I join in as well. It's fun, so much fun, I tell you.

The linden tree says:

I like the old people especially, but I like children, too. In the summer an old man comes to me every day, you have all seen him. He walks very slowly with a cane and is happy when he can sit on the bench next to me. Then he sits there quietly and thinks back on the many years of his life. Everything that the old man sees in his soul I see with him. I know what he looked like as a young man and as a boy, and I know everything he has done. Sometimes a mother comes, too, with a small child in her arms, sits on the bench and nurses the little one. By the way, have you noticed that my wide body is hollow on the bottom? At noon, when it is very hot, two little children often come to me; a brother and sister. They take each other by the hand, crawl all the way inside me and sleep in my lap. I shelter them. I hear them breathe. Their dreams drift up to me, and I live in them. You know, that is the most beautiful experience I can ever have.

The oak tree says:

I like the strong, brave, wild children! Especially the boys! But the little girls, too, if they are not too prissy. I call to the boys: Hey, you over there, don't be such lazybones. Are you cowards? Grab each other, have at it, and let's see who's the strongest. Then the boys light into each other, grab one another by the pants and collars, wrestling and swinging so it's a joy to behold. That is fun, I'm telling you! When one of them gets knocked down I call to him: Hey, do you want to lie on the ground forever? Are you a weakling? Have you lost your nerve already? No? Then stand up, take a deep breath and try again. This time you'll be the champion, for sure! Just never give up! Yes, that's how I call to the children, so that they become brave. The world has no use for weaklings.

It almost goes without saying that the children also want to draw and paint the trees. The pictures proved to be very interesting. How appropriate was the melancholic child's drawing of the weeping willow. How airy and sweet the sanguine child drew the birch. How powerful was the choleric child's picture of the oak, with fiery lightning and black clouds. How broad and unformed the phlegmatic child drew the linden. But also, how comical the sanguine child's first attempt to draw the weeping willow came out. Quite against the child's will it became a merry little tree, which lets its twigs flutter saucily in the wind. The children soon learned, however, to draw each of the four trees (and others as well) according to its inner nature, for they approached each and every one with love.

The Legitimate Path of Teaching

Questions concerning the goal of education have existed ever since education was first practiced, written about and discussed. This goal is formulated in pedagogical literature in the most diverse ways. Reading this literature (from the obsolete to the brand new), one can make the following discovery: Despite their great variety, these educational goals, are *so* great and lofty, that one could adopt most of them without reservation.

Rudolf Steiner says that the teacher's job is to instill in children the ability to cope with life. With these simple, almost simplistic sounding words, he, too, advances an educational goal. Is there a single teacher who could not adopt such a goal? What teacher would want the children leaving his classroom to be unable to cope with life? It does not seem all that difficult for teachers to agree on a goal of education.

But what about the path leading to this goal? You need not look very far to discover that the paths diverge greatly, seemingly leading to different goals altogether. It soon becomes apparent that the noble words about the goal of education must remain no more than words, if the knowledge of spiritual laws, in particular the laws of development that are active in the growing child, is lacking. Once these laws of development are understood, the right direction and path will become apparent. The right path is of the utmost importance. The teacher who lacks knowledge of the spiritual laws of development sets off on the wrong path. It may lead to momentary success, but it will fall short of the goal of education: true ability to cope with life, and not merely with life's daily routine.

If we disregard nuances and transition phases, two methods (or paths) of teaching predominate in practical education today. I would like to juxtapose them in a somewhat radical way.

The first method seeks to fill the child with the greatest possible amount of knowledge in the shortest possible time. It pushes directly toward the goal of outwardly visible success. The methods devised for making something plausible to the child are sophisticated and even admirable. The faster a child can make use of his knowledge or abilities, the better the method looks. When a five-year-old child has learned to read in twenty days, it is publicized as a crowning achievement. All measures are aimed at attaining immediate success. This is the most short-sighted approach to education because, despite theoretical arguments to the contrary, the teaching material is purely an end in itself. Many of the various "experimental reforms" are, upon closer inspection, nothing but improvements on this kind of shortcut. They seek to reach still more quickly what once required several important steps.

A teacher utilizing the second method asks himself in everything he does: How does this affect the child in body and soul? He says to himself, Everything I think and do in my class, yes, my entire being, influences the growing human being. Either I damage him (even if the damage is not immediately apparent) or I succeed in unlocking the soul's forces in him. I can corrupt or I can heal, but no part of my being is without impact on the child. Because the teacher is aware of the nature of the child and his hidden laws of development, his goal cannot be to devise a clever method of cramming the children with the greatest possible amount of testable knowledge in the shortest possible time.

He would have to be under pressure from outside constraints since he knows that such an approach can damage the child in a way from which the child will probably never recover. However, he does not belittle the teaching material, for this is his tool for strengthening the child in soul and spirit, of making him able to cope with life. But he knows that the famous and still highly acclaimed school goal of sending the child out into the world with a head full of intellectual knowledge may weigh him down like a millstone around his neck. Therefore, the teacher does not choose the shortcut. On the contrary, he chooses what may appear to be actual detours over the streamlined approach. But where do these "detours" lead? They lead to the souls of the children, for it is these which the teacher wishes to reach and bring into full bloom. Upon closer examination it is precisely this "round-about" path that proves to be the real and therefore legitimate path of teaching.

In order to explain and amplify what has just been discussed I have selected a few examples from the reading and writing and arithmetic classes.

The detours through the child's soul can be seen most clearly in the very first writing class, or in the way the child is taught to read and write today's conventional letters. Since I have already discussed the first writing class to some extent in this book, I will allow myself to touch only briefly on the essential aspects of it now, in order to spend more time on a different example. To begin with, the path that leads the child to the letters *T* and *K* is very long (as the reader will remember). First, the child internalizes the living image of the King's fight with the troll. Then this fight is brought to life with paintbrush and watercolors or with colored pencils. Little by little this picture is transformed as the living picture gradually disappears and only the naked skeletons of the letters *T* and *K* remain. Without a doubt, these are valid forms in which the intellect expresses itself, but if they have not been derived from living imagery, they must remain foreign to the child. How different from this path is the other, seemingly rational method. It takes the modern letters as they have emerged today after a long development and, heedless of their origin, uses amazing ingenuity to introduce them to the child as such. Then the child is taught, often in an amazingly short period of time, to manipulate the letters. But this is a superficial activity, for the child has not been given the opportunity to develop an inner connection to them. And how could he have developed his soul forces on these letter skeletons? In a few weeks, however, the child has thus learned to juggle things that he has never experienced, that are more like ghosts to him than living, merry and friendly beings. In other words, he has learned to read.

It does not seem to require excessive clairvoyance to see that this shortcut, because it considers neither the nature of the child's soul nor the long path covered by all mankind, cannot be the legitimate path of the educator. It can never prepare the child to cope with life in the true sense of the words.

Further accounts of the writing class consistently revealed that although the legitimate path appears to be more roundabout than the other—because it takes certain laws into account—it is nevertheless the path for the true educator to follow.

It follows that the teacher will also want to avoid introducing the child abruptly to the uncapitalized, small letters. Instead, he will provide the child with the experience of recognizing them from their origins. The small letters stem from the capital letters the way daughters do from mothers. The little ones have developed out of the big ones through various delightful changes. If the child recognizes the origin of the small letters, and if he is allowed to participate in the transformations in a quasi-dramatic way, then he comes to love the little forms, for his soul has made the inner connection to them. The child then might say, "This is the mommy and these are her babies. But lots of times the babies don't look like their mommy one bit, but I know they belong together because I watched the baby come from its mommy with my own eyes. Then some babies look so much like their mommy that you wouldn't be able to tell them apart if they weren't a little smaller. It's kind of boring, though, when the babies look exactly like their mommy, and haven't even tried to be a little different."

The long path from the capital mother letters to the little baby letters (the path that took so much "valuable time") was worth it. The children speak of the small letters as beings that they love, because their soul was able to flourish in them.

I would like to use a second example from the reading and writing class to illustrate my point. The German language has not only the Roman but also the Gothic printed letters. What adult would be incapable of using them? Any educated person can read them. But what if the adult uses these letters as a vehicle without recognizing their nature or understanding their being? Try writing them! Anyone can read a Gothic letter, particularly if it is part of a written word. But has he internalized the letters so that he can freely reproduce and write them? From what I have observed, the answer is almost always no. He begins, hesitates, stops and admits with embarrassment and amazement at himself that he cannot do it. Yes, that is the way it goes. We make use of certain symbols without knowing their nature because we have no inner connection to them. We arrive at the serious insight that these symbols lead a ghostly existence in us, for we are conscious neither of their true form nor of their origin. We live with many such ghosts; they do not unfold our soul forces, so they rumble about inside us all the more. Examples of such ghosts are the many modern means of transportation (tramway or streetcar), to the extent we use them without knowing how they operate. On this subject Rudolf Steiner says the following: "We use the tools of civilization nowadays . . . without having the slightest idea of what is behind them. This largely explains why we have become such a tense species. When we are constantly surrounded by situations we do not understand, we become confused, even if this confusion is purely subconscious." (*Menschenschule*, June, Year 4, p. 170.)

What Rudolf Steiner says about streetcars and similar products of civilization applies also, I believe, to today's letters, particularly the Gothic printed letters. If they are not understood, they confuse our subconscious. Just as it is necessary for a 14-year-old to gain real insight into how a streetcar can move without being visibly pulled, so it is necessary for an eight- or nine-year-old to experience how the Gothic printed letters, which to a certain extent are also a vehicle, came into being. A child will understand what something is if he knows how it came to be. In fact, it can even be of noticeable benefit to the adult to become conscious of the origin and nature of these symbols, in the same way that understanding the technical secret of the electronically driven train acts as a soothing balm. Both are preconditions for truly being able to cope with life.

The teacher must not regret the "valuable time" and the "long path" necessary to lead the children to such an experience. Therefore he will avoid introducing the children to these printed forms abruptly, but will show them gradually how these forms developed out of the simple Roman letters through numerous transformations. In this way the unadorned starting form will shine through the oddest, most embellished, most ornate end-product. Next, the

teacher will let the children draw or paint these very compli-
cated letters, but on big sheets of paper and as large as possible, so that the form becomes clearly visible. In this way the
child understands the signs and masters them. Of course,
from the short-sighted, pedantic point of view you lose time
with such an approach, but the fact remains that it is the
real, and therefore legitimate, path.

There are times, however, when it is extraordinarily difficult for the teacher to find the legitimate path. For example, in teaching the children how to spell according to current
rules of orthography, a very topical problem. Most teachers
realize that today's spelling is something very "human,"
which is not the result of old, sacred traditions, that on the
contrary, it is an expression of a fairly recent obsession with
flourishes and embellishments. Should the teacher, by
beginning at the beginning, once again let the children walk
the same path as some of their ancestors did, and in so doing
show how wonderfully far we have come with today's spelling standards?

This is perhaps a particularly difficult case, in which imposing the conventional system on the children really seems
unavoidable. Perhaps in the beginning, moved by compassion, the teacher will allow the children some freedom in
how they write words, only to place them under the yoke of
spelling soon after.

Rudolf Steiner often pointed out that when it comes to
spelling the teacher must guard primarily against presenting
the rules of spelling as divine law. In other words, never say,
"This is how it is written according to holy decree." Always
say, "This is how it is written by adults." There is a fundamental difference here from an educational point of view. In
the first case, a completely false and therefore disastrous
faith in authority is being cultivated. In the second case, the
child feels from the beginning that what we are dealing with

here is merely a convention among people to write words in the same way. A false faith in authority haunts our age, and it is no less serious if people are often totally unaware of it. This unrecognized misplaced faith also contributes to the inability to cope with life.

It is necessary, then, for the teacher to awaken the feeling in his pupils that writing correctly is only a matter of observing an outer form, a convention. Rudolf Steiner's comments on fractions (*Menschenschule*, June, Year 4, p. 168) also apply to spelling: "Some of the false faith in authority would fade if right from the beginning everything that is actually based on a convention were introduced to the child's emotions as such, as things determined by convention."

I must confess, however, that the children prompted me to take at least a small step along the legitimate path. It happened like this: While learning about the biblical story of creation, the children had learned the Wessobrunner Prayer by heart, and what made a particularly strong impression on them was the Old High German in the original text. After they knew the verse by heart, they also wanted to know how it was written. I then wrote the text on the board the way I had found it in Braune (Old High German Reader, p. 82). The first few lines of this verse on the beginning of the world read follows:

> Dat gafregin ih mit firahim firiuuizzo meista
> Dat ero niuuas noh ûfhimil,
> noh paum noh pereg ni uuas
> ni sterro noheinîg noh sunna ni sce in
> noh mâno ni liuhta, noh der mârea sêo.

The children were astonished by the strange script and spelling. For a while they were quite still, but then they started: "There are no words with *ie* in them, or with two *o*'s or two *a*'s or two *e*'s. But all the long *o*'s and *a*'s have the

same little hat on. And all of the words start with little letters, even the tree or the mountain or the sea; even the sun
and the moon have little letters . . ."³ Then it was still again
for a while. All of a sudden a little girl's face lit up with
understanding. One moment she had her mouth open, without speaking, and the next she said (her voice full of utter
amazement), "People had a much smarter way of writing back
then than they do now!"—All children agreed. I then asked
them, "Should I now teach you to write all words the way
they are spelled on the blackboard, where all long vowels
simply have a little hat, and where all words, even God and
the angels, are written small, all of which you think is so
smart? Or should I teach you to write words the way all
adults do today?" I admit, I held my breath while I waited
for the answer. What would I do if the children opted for
the old writing method? Utter silence reigned again for a
while, but then they all said, "No, we want to learn to write
the way grown-ups do today." From now on the children
wrote "consciously," the way adults usually do, although it
is not nearly so smart. The deep need of the child to imitate
the adult in all ways had won out.

What has been said about the writing lesson also goes for
the arithmetic lesson. Here, too, there is a legitimate (real)
and as it were illegitimate (abstract) path. In a previous
chapter I have described in great detail how to introduce
children to arithmetic. I also indicated there how long the
path is that finally leads the children to the addition $1 + 1 = 2$.
Where I end the journey others quite illegitimately begin. I
expressed this approximately as follows: What should stand
on its feet is stood on its head, because adults, who are ruled
primarily by the head, fail to realize that the legitimate path
of the child can only go from the limbs and heart up to the
head, and not the other way around. I would now like to ex-
pand on my previous statements with another small example.

When the children approach their ninth year, they must be introduced to the world of measures, weights, coins and clock-time. Only the meter is still considered a valid linear measure in Switzerland. What kind of measure is the meter? Where did it come from? Was it given to ancient man by the gods as a particularly sacred gift? The answers to these questions can easily be found in the encyclopedia. The meter was established as a mere convention in 1799 at the time of the French Revolution. The "standard meter," made of platinum (which has a very small expansion coefficient), is deposited in the National Archives in Paris. Despite the fact that this standard meter is visible and can even be touched by those trusted not to run off with it, the meter is completely non-human, a mere abstraction. What do humanity and the human body have to do with the meter? Nothing. This artificially established standard, however, has proven very useful. Contrary to so many other innovations of the French Revolution, the meter remains an essential tool to this very day, and for now there is no reason to abandon it.

But is that any reason why the child should be introduced to this cleverly thought out measure in one fell swoop? I believe that as teachers, we must take the human, legitimate path, a path via mankind, for man himself is the most legitimate work of creation. He is the first and noblest measure of all things.

With his legs he measures the earth in strides.
With his feet he walks the earth.
He stretches out his arms.
He stands on the earth as a complete being.

Yes, man can use his legs and feet, his arms and hands, in fact his entire body as a measure. The parts of the body are truly the measures that man can most call his own; they are not abstract, but concrete. When measuring with such measures man, himself is present. His awareness of the body gives him the awareness of measure, and each measurement renews and heightens his awareness.

It is extremely important that the children become aware of, and learn to use, the measures built into their body. The child should feel down to his fingertips and toes, This is my stride, this is my arm's length, this is my foot, this is the span of my two fingers, this is my armbone, and it goes from my elbow down to the longest fingertip. The teacher does the child a favor if he allows him to measure the things in his environment with his own units of measure for a few days.

Soon the child begins to notice that his measures are not rigid and unchanging. He can, for example, make long strides and shorter ones, the finger span is also a flexible measure. The child even may discover on his own, In one year my armbone will be a little bigger than it is today, and I will get to school faster because my legs will be longer. While the child feels and predicts the growth of his limbs, he also notices the world with new measures. He experiences himself in all his aliveness.

Soon the children notice something else as well, and they say to one another, "My step isn't the same as yours. I have bigger feet than you do. There are Tommy-steps and Billy-steps, as many kinds of steps as there are kids in the class or people in the world." The child discovers that everyone has his own measure with which he experiences the world; he senses that everyone is an individual. The specter of collective man is banished.

Thus, in the interest of accuracy it is incorrect to say, Our classroom is five strides long. You might be able to say it is five Tommy-steps long (but Billy, because he is smaller, must take six steps). "How high is our classroom?" I asked. That was a bit hard to measure since the children could not reach the ceiling. So, I stood one boy against the wall, a second one climbed onto his shoulders, and what do you know, with his longest fingertip he could just reach the ceiling. But again you could not say, "Our room is as high as can be reached by the fingertip of one boy standing on another's shoulders." We felt it would be more precise to say, "When Tommy in the third grade climbs on Billy's shoulders, who is also in the third grade, he can just touch the ceiling."

The children also experienced: We may be the measure of all things, but sometimes it is a bit tricky. Each person has his own measures and, on top of that, these undergo transformations within the same person, particularly when he is still young. What can be done about it? Well, that is why the grown-ups agreed to kill these measures so that they could no longer grow. The human measures were frozen (standardized). Now every ell[4] is the same because people want it that way (it suits them better), exactly such and such a length, not longer and not shorter. All ells in the whole world are now the same length. They have become a little boring along the way, but they can still be rather useful.

But why three or even more measures of length instead of just one? Now comes the leap away from man into empty abstraction; it is the leap from the ell, the span, the foot (all of which still carry human traces even as standardized measures), to the meter, which is not a human (but also not a heavenly) measure. The meter is a conventional measure and had to be clearly presented as such, but only after a lengthy introduction.

Nonetheless, we must try to relate the meter to the human body, to link the abstract with the concrete. How long is a meter? As long as two of Tommy's steps, or as long as four of his feet, or seven of Melissa's finger spans, etc. The children also learned to "make" the meter their own within one finger width's accuracy. Thus the meter was measured on the individual human measures. Eventually, once it was recognized and understood, we graciously put it to work in our service.

What has been discussed here regarding linear measures could be similarly presented for the other measures, especially money, the classic invention for the sake of human convenience. Instead of telling the children that a plow costs so and so many dollars, let them (and this is just to give you a hint in which direction to go) think about what the farmer must give to the blacksmith, in vegetables or livestock, to pay him for his labor and expenses. One child said to me, "The farmer must give the blacksmith a sack of potatoes for the plow." Another said ten sacks of potatoes, a third said an old horse, and a fourth said a billy-goat and a baby goat. We can see how such questions lead from the abstract to the concrete.

Teaching the children about how the day is divided into two sequences of twelve hours requires special care and quite a long path. What an immense difference exists between the movement of the stars in the sky or the course of the sun around the earth—both guided by divine spirits—and the ticking of two hands around a clock, driven by a spring in the casing!

Are not the sun, moon and stars, from the perspective of a clock hand, making huge detours? But who could deny that these detours are the legitimate paths, the life-giving ones, and that they lead to the true goal?

Unscheduled Classroom Events

There is a vast amount of pedagogical literature with which the teacher can further his professional education. But no matter how carefully he selects his reading material, he will always come away with the feeling: This is nothing but words and theory. If I don't want it to weigh me down, I had better forget about it while I'm teaching. And the teacher is lucky if, during his interaction with the children, he can forget everything he has learned in books. Even Rudolf Steiner's educational writings, as ungrateful as this may seem, must be suppressed in front of the child, even though their innermost essence is vastly superior to that of standard pedagogical literature. The difference between Rudolf Steiner's writings and standard writings is this: Standard writings must by their very nature *remain* theory, whereas Rudolf Steiner's writings have the power to awaken in the reader something that can lead to pedagogical intuitions. If the reader shows inner readiness, Rudolf Steiner's writings on education can become "books of initiation"; they are a path by which the teacher can transform his own being. Then he no longer says to himself: I have once again learned something new about teaching. I have to hurry and find out if this new knowledge works, today if possible, so that I don't forget it. Instead he might feel: Something has come to life inside me that was "dead" before. It gives me the courage to teach. True, I may be far from being a teacher, but a spark of the teacher's fire has begun to glow.

Becoming a teacher does not mean reading up on education. It means (and this comes from studying Rudolf Steiner's writings properly) walking a long and difficult path of knowledge. What are the many milestones lined up along this path? They are the countless mistakes that the teacher makes, which burden his own destiny and that of the children.

Still, once the teacher has taken at least one step along this path of knowledge, how changed the world of the child —so often evoked as cliché—looks to him then. He must say to himself: Before, you were completely blind, now you begin to see, to wake up. You see subtleties in the child that went unnoticed before, how his hand moves, how he walks, how his fingernails grow, how his ears are formed, how often the color of his face or the tone of his voice changes in a single morning. The teacher is then on the way to an understanding of the child.

And what of the small schoolchild? It is as if he wanted to probe the teacher with fine, psychic touch organs. He senses that something wants to approach him and form a bond. He looks beyond what is still "dead" and forms a direct bond with what has already come to "life" in the teacher. Now the child has absolutely no reason not to put a natural trust in his teachers. Now he gives himself the way he is.

He has no reason to play a part, to try to appear more virtuous than he is. He also does not retreat into a shell, living in his own special world in a way completely foreign to the teacher. The relationship of teacher and child undergoes a fundamental change. The child does not hold back in word or deed. He stands before the teacher without inhibitions, creating the atmosphere without which true education (and not mere instruction) would be impossible. It is up to the teacher to create and nurture this vital educational environment.

In such an atmosphere it goes without saying that the children like to talk about what they have experienced, or tell their own stories, "poems," dreams of the previous night, etc. Nor do they hold back during class time (I am referring to children younger than nine) from expressing what strongly engages their souls; they come right out with it. Often this creates quite an interesting situation for the teacher, but it makes demands on his teaching creativity to which he may not always be equal. During such a class, the situation is constantly changing, and the teacher must know how to make each new situation an educational experience. He may face situations that could not arise anywhere else (because of limits set by prescribed and mandatory school regulations), situations that would end in "catastrophe" if at that moment you tried to guide yourself by one of Rudolf Steiner's lectures about a similar situation, rather than acting out of the consciousness awakened by these lectures.

I would like to continue by relating a few teaching "incidents" in order to illustrate what I have just touched on. This kind of "telling tales out of school" only makes sense, however, if it describes a way of teaching or, more specifically, characterizes the relationship of the children to their teacher better than the most thorough treatise. Publishing school anecdotes merely for the sake of entertainment I gladly leave to the many writers of light fiction.

As an introduction I have chosen two short poems by a child with a very rich and active imagination. Keep in mind, however, that for small children content is only of secondary importance, and that it is rather in the rhythmic element that he wishes to express himself. You should have seen and heard the child recite his poem, how he moved his head back and forth and could not keep his feet still, or how emphatically he put the accent on certain syllables.

Sigh wind sigh,	Sigh wind sigh
Rock our little child,	Rock our little child,
Rock him in the sunshine,	Do not rock him in the rain,
Oh he likes that so fine.	That gives our baby pain.

or: I am sure,
        My heart is pure.
        I am lazy,
        I am crazy.
        I am dead,
        My heart is red.

It is particularly in the second little poem, which is virtually meaningless, that the child's real love of rhythm and also his love of rhyme are displayed.

The children frequently tell their dreams, too, be it to the teacher alone (which happens rarely) or to the whole class. I have chosen four of the dreams related to me, two of which will weigh heavily on the teacher's mind, I know. I am passing them along to you anyway because I believe they are illustrative. Through dreams the children not only express their liking for the teacher (which really happens from time to time), but also tell him that he has been unjust or is blind to the dangerous situation in which they find themselves. Such a dream can then open the unsuspecting teacher's eyes to what he must do, which he should have done a long time ago.

The following two dreams were told by the same child. I should add that it is my *own* child, whom I also teach in school. Since the child told both these dreams completely without inhibition in front of the whole class, I see no reason why they should not be cited here. The child related as follows: "I was in bed, all alone, no one was there. Then my father climbed into bed with me and waved his hand in all directions. From everywhere he had waved his hand came angels in beautiful clothes and with golden wings. They came from all sides until there was a big crowd, and all the angels stood around us."

Only a few weeks later, however, the same child told a

second dream in school: "My father and I and Eveli (her younger sister) were flying in an airplane over lots of water. But my father would look at and talk only to Eveli and didn't pay any attention to me. Then I fell out of the plane into the water and I kept yelling, 'Daddy, Daddy'—But he didn't hear me. Then I woke up."

The dream's message was clear and could no longer go unheard.

A boy who always had to struggle with arithmetic once handed me his notebook at the end of an arithmetic class and asked, "Did I get all the problems right?" I hastily glanced over the problems, thought I found some mistakes and said, "A few are not right." At this the boy returned to his desk quite crestfallen. That evening I looked at the notebook again and discovered that I had been wrong. I felt terrible about disappointing the child as a result of my own error. I thought, If I could only tell him right now that all the problems are right. But tomorrow I will tell him first thing.—The next morning the boy came bounding up to me and said, "Last night I had a great dream, do you want to hear it?" And then he reported, "I dreamed that school was over for the day. First I played outside, but later my mother called me in and said that I had done all the arithmetic problems wrong. But after a while she called me again and said the problems were all right after all. Boy, was I happy!"— Now I could tell the child that his dream was true.

How sweetly the short dream of a little girl expresses her love for her English teacher: "I dreamed we were having English with Mrs. X. That was great! Then all of a sudden Mrs. X. turned into a beautiful princess."

The following are a few remarks by children that are appropriate at this point. They are meant primarily to illustrate the children's lack of inhibitions. I do not think, however, that it would serve any purpose for me to say what my answers were, or how I "behaved." What I did each time was exceedingly important for myself and my children, but is without significance for anyone else. Needless to say, no matter how dismal the situation, the teacher tries to salvage what is best for the child.

In a writing class I once said to a little girl, "Listen, you are not writing at all well today." I watched as a dark cloud passed over her face. This particular child was strongly dominated by her melancholic temperament, but also had a streak of defiance. After the class she took my hand and we walked side by side for a while without speaking. I noticed that something had come between us, like a little wall. Suddenly the little girl looked at me and said, "Well, you know, it's better to write badly than not to live at all." This remark full of the defiant will to live pleased me all the more at the time as that same child had said to me a few days earlier, "It's not at all nice in this world, no, not one little bit nice." Through my reproach the world-weary mood of the little girl had been transformed into a valiant will to live!

A little boy behaved quite differently when I said to him, "Listen, your penmanship is really awful. Look how wild your letters are." He put his pen aside, looked at me in a very friendly way and said, "Yes, well, you and I we don't have the same taste." I must emphasize that the little boy is an extraordinarily polite and sweet child, and that these words contained no trace of impudence.

It is most interesting and instructive to observe how long a child addresses his teacher with the familiar *Du* (the German informal *you*). When, in what moment, in what situation does the *Du* give way to the *Sie* (the German formal "you"), only to suddenly reappear, and then disappear permanently at some other time? There was a little boy in my class who completely failed to notice during his first two years in school that other children in his class had already chosen the sophisticated *Sie*-form of address. One day, I remember it well, he began to prick up his ears when another child addressed me with *Sie*. His face expressed complete amazement, and he became very shy for a time and avoided speaking to me. Then one morning—it was very quiet in the classroom —he called out with complete ease and in a tone of benevolent command, "Mein lieber Herr Aeppli, kommen *Sie* bitte gleich zu mir und *zeig* [*Du*-form of the verb] mir, wie ich es machen soll." (My dear Mr. Aeppli, please come here right away and show me how to do it.) The *Sie* resounded powerfully around the room. It was a big step into the world! The little boy was fairly bursting with joy all morning because of this crowning achievement in chic elegance.

The same child (before this *Sie* episode) was picked on by another by during recess. His eyes swam with tears as he came into the classroom, and I could not help feeling rather sorry for him. Even after everyone else had been drawing for quite some time he still nursed his grievance. Finally he got everything off his chest with these words: "The teacher makes school as beautiful as Paradise for us, but as for M., he makes it as horrible as hell." The boy's black and white portrayal was a success. The other children laughed, not at the boy who had been picked on, but at the blackened and branded bully. The nasty business ended well without my having to interfere, because a child was allowed to put his feelings into words openly and without inhibition. The same pedagogical result simply cannot be achieved using the "children should be seen and not heard" method, which cannot in itself be an educational tool. But aside from the fact that being seen and heard is beneficial to the small child, the words that are called forth from the emotional soul of the child, the unhibited remarks, are both valuable pathfinders for the teacher and informative glimpses into the milieu of the child.

How much is expressed, for example, in the following "judgment" of an eight-year-old girl during a painting class. The children were painting lots of angels, but for one little boy they just would not turn out. His main problem was that he kept forgetting to give his angels wings. Finally he made his misfortune public: "I still haven't painted a real angel, just an ordinary lady." To which a little girl replied (without even raising her eyes from her own work): "Yes, well, you're just going to have to learn that a lady is never an angel and an angel is never a lady."

I want to leave you with this one last picture: I told the children the story of the Fall of Man. The children were visibly moved as they listened, and pretty soon were unable to hold back their own opinions. Each child wanted to say what he or she would have done as Eve. I want to pass on three of these comments, and I believe they reflect the different inner personalities of the three children. The first child stood up, face glowing with pure, righteous anger, and exclaimed full of true fighting spirit: "I would have taken an ax, fought with the serpent and killed it." He accompanied these words with a wrathful swing of his arm. The second child looked at me trustingly and said, "I wouldn't have taken the apple at all." The third child, however, after all the other children had had their say, said, "I would have taken a bite of the apple, but then I would have turned the bitten apple around and hung it so cleverly back on the tree that God would never have noticed that there was a bite out of it."

This concludes my small series of teaching vignettes. I feel compelled, though, to stress once more that I have not related these examples merely for their own sake, but to illustrate the thoughts outlined in the introduction.

Transforming the Subject Matter

Consider the following entirely plausible situation: A teacher, unaware of anthroposophy, but equipped with a healthy intellect and a critical eye, decides to get to the bottom of things. This teacher also wants to be able to justify all his actions in his own mind. Moreover, he still has a fairly unspoiled sensitivity for what is healthy or sick, straight or crooked. Yet, it is precisely this natural ability that causes him problems. He lacks the intellectual basis to prove much of what he feels is undeniably right or wrong. This causes an inner conflict in the teacher, which does not make his life any easier. It forces him to live in a state of constant inner turmoil, but thus also prevents complacency and false intellectual modesty. It makes him a *searcher*. What is he searching for? For the meaning of life. Since, however, he is not only a man, but also a teacher, his search is narrowed down from the meaning of life to the meaning of education.

This teacher says to himself, Do I go to school every day in order to teach? Am I only trying to make a living? Is it a last resort because I am not fit for any other job? Or is my job more of a vocation after all? Whatever the case may be, I will not rest until I have discovered the meaning of education. I feel that there is meaning there, but I lack the strength to turn that feeling into a clear thought. But perhaps others are more informed than I and have long been clear on the meaning of all education.

Our teacher now eagerly and conscientiously reads books and magazines on education. He divorces himself from all religious or other ties. I will take what is good no matter what the source, he says to himself frequently. One day the annual report of a teacher training institute falls into his hands. In it he finds a piece on the "meaning and nature of Christian education." His interest aroused, the teacher enthusiastically begins to read. He becomes more and more pensive, however, and after reading a particular sentence he must stop and ask himself, Am I reading this correctly?

> In short, *evangelical education* at every age level is first a process of tearing down what man's proud self-consciousness has erected. But because man can so easily take pleasure in destruction, it is exactly the evangelical teacher who must guard against enjoying tearing things down. He must speak not only of God's wrath, but also of His grace.

What? Education is "first" supposed to be a tearing down? The gardener grows roses and asters, the farmer raises calves. Only the teacher, because he does not deal with flowers and calves, is supposed to destroy. What would such a Christian seminar director think was the actual educational work of a teacher? A strange give and take! With one hand the teacher is supposed to take away from the child the basis of his human worth: the potential of his self. With the other hand, however, he is supposed to give the child something of dubious value: God's grace as rigid dogma.

No, says the teacher, I will not go along with that, no matter how subtly the latest theology tries to prove the validity of that approach.

To balance things out, the teacher now reads something that seems to stem from a completely different branch of educational thought. The source is a journal published by an institute that studies current questions on education and instruction. The question under discussion in this issue is, Teacher or machine? The following quote is where our teacher once again gets stuck:

The *record and cylinder* (of the tape recorder) have a great advantage over the living teacher: you can repeat a sentence or a word as often as you like. The pronunciation, intonation and speed of the speaker are thereby not only conveyed to the unknown listener (the child, that is) but are also indelibly impressed upon him. Only a machine always speaks the same way.

What is this view of life telling me, our teacher asks himself? Why, that adults tend to do without education entirely! The teacher is to be replaced by the machine and its obvious advantages, first only partially, of course, but then completely. What is the give and take now? What is being taken from the child? The living human being and the teacher. And what does he receive in exchange? That which the machine indelibly impresses upon his soul through constant repetition. As before, the child is robbed of something precious and given a gift of highly dubious value. No, I cannot go along with this any more than I could with the other.

Through a lucky coincidence the teacher now stumbles upon the educational writings of Paul Vital Troxler. At last, he calls out as he reads, something that really interests me as a teacher and is also very relevant to the current situation! He completely forgets that these words were written a hundred and fifty years ago, a time when there were no such things as psychoanalysis and experimental psychology.

In Troxler he finds these words on the essence of education:

He who puts himself in someone else's hands to be educated offers up the greatest possible sacrifice, namely himself, with all his gifts, and with his entire future. He therefore has the right to demand that through the teacher his own self be returned to him. Indeed, the condition of his apparent self-relinquishment is that he may become stronger and truer to himself, so that he may achieve his original, natural destiny and his freedom of choice more securely and happily. Thus, education should neither give nor take, but simply guide man back to his true nature, which, in turn, is revealed only by his liberated education . . . Only God can truly reach, and true education is nothing but releasing and freeing.

Out of these words speaks insight into the true nature of education, thinks the teacher. My instinct says yes to these words. What a find I have made. Education means neither giving nor taking, but releasing and freeing.

Now, however, I am faced with a new problem. It is clear to me that I have nothing to take from the child. I cannot take away his potential and I cannot remove myself as his teacher. As for the giving, do I not give the child a daily dose of subject matter as his mother gives him his daily vitamin? Is there a secret here that is not yet visible to me, like the one Angelus Silesius spoke of?

> Bread does not nourish thee
> It is what bread has in it
> God's eternal Word,
> Its life and its spirit.

Do I just think I am giving something, something which the way I intend it is not even right? I am going to do everything I can to understand the secret of the subject matter. I am sure it will be worth it. The search for the meaning of education leads me to investigate the meaning of the subject matter. The scope of the problem seems to be steadily shrinking. I am beginning to suspect that the great secret of education contains two other secrets. First, the child I have before me. Second, the subject matter that I have to "give" the child. Both riddles must be "solved" by one and the same individual, namely myself.

Now the teacher pursues the nature of the subject matter. To reach this end he asks himself a few seemingly simplistic questions. For example: who supplies me with the subject matter that I need in my lessons? I teach botany and zoology and I "take" my material from the plants that grow out of the earth, and from the animals that run over the earth. In order to teach world history I must refer to the deeds of bygone men; they supply me with the subject matter. And the language that men speak allows me to teach grammar.

Why do I use this subject matter in my lessons? Of course, it is prescribed by the state, and I do what all other teachers do. But would I not do it on my own, out of my own insight, as it were? Certainly I would, for if being born into this world has any meaning at all, it is to learn about the world and to work in it. The subjects help me accomplish this. Here is the child; there is the world. Between them stands the teacher, at least for a few hours a day. He is meant to be the mediator, the one who opens doors for the child, and each subject is a door to the world.

But first I must know the world myself. I must be able to open the doors for myself, of course. Have I opened them? Or for that matter, how do I experience the environment that has been kind enough to "supply" me with the subject matter? Now I see: the narrow question of the subject matter suddenly leads me out into the world.

At the question, How do I experience the environment myself, the teacher begins to be confused. The following thoughts go through his mind: I take a specific plant and study it. I look at the number and form of the flower petals, examine the stem, make cross-sections of the leaf stalks and roots, pore over it inch by inch with a microscope. Have I understood it? No!

I find the flower beautiful. Could that be the first step towards understanding? It pleases me, and I take it home.

Does that mean I understand it better? No. Its life is a mystery to me, it eludes me; in the end I am left only with wilted leaves and a stalk, not a plant. I do not share in its growth and blooming. It seems to belong to a completely different world.

Over there is an animal. I can see it quite distinctly. I see its fur, its eyes, its head. I hear its animal cry, as well. Yet it runs away right under my nose. I love a dog; I am full of compassion for him, so I pet him and give him table scraps. Does that mean I understand his makeup and breed? No. We might as well be separated by an abyss.

How can I understand history? How can I gain a living understanding for the deeds of a bygone age without having been there myself? I do not even understand myself and my own language, which really ought to be a part of me.

One thing I do know now: What I can grasp is not reality and, therefore, is also not what is at work underneath. In relation to what I sense to be reality, what I grasp is unreal and ineffective. I am supposed to pass subject matter on to the child that has become devoid of effect. What a fate! But is that my *individual* fate?

There are richly endowed collections of subject matter, vast storerooms in which everything that the teacher needs is neatly and systematically stacked. These are the books "at the teacher's disposal." So efficiently is the enormous amount of material organized there that often just thinking about it is enough to convince you that grammar, world history, botany and zoology exist only in books. Behind the books, however, stand the authors. I may not know them personally, but they are certainly just as human as I am. What do these books, behind which stand the authors, mirror? They mirror the bleak reflection of their own bleak reality. Here are the books on nature, and there is living nature. The books approach the plant and animal kingdoms in the same way because the authors cannot penetrate the essential nature of either one. What is the result? The stuffed animal and the pressed flower.—On one side is the speech of living men, on the other side is grammar as described in books, and which, if you are not careful, can become an instrument of torture for children; a grammar of grotesque exercises with the express purpose of obliterating all joy in human speech.

Similarly, there are the deeds and passions of a race, and here is history as an endless collection of facts. What disturbing things *Nietzsche* had to say of history. It was compiled in excess in order to ruin man. It has robbed men of their humanity and through a horrible metamorphosis has changed them into flesh-and-blood compendia, into walking encyclopedias. History means more to Nietzsche, however, than merely a particular scientific or educational field. For him, the way history reveals itself unambiguously in historical science and history classes is both a way of thinking and a research and teaching method. This "history" has filled man with a "huge quantity of indigestible stones of knowledge, which then, (. . .) can sometimes be heard rumbling about inside him."[5]

"An enormous mass of knowledge, unable to be a life-giving influence on the one hand, and a barbarous influence on the other, these are the effects of history," says Nietzsche. "History," he says, "can be borne only by strong personalities; weak ones are utterly extinguished by it."[6] How terrible the effect of this history must be on children, who are neither strong nor weak personalities, but who, with the teacher's help, still want to become personalities.

No, says the teacher to himself, history has become dead matter. It can only extinguish life, it cannot kindle strength. Nietzsche's battle is not with a field, however, but with a way of thinking, namely my own and that of my contemporaries. It assaults me from the pages of every book, whether it be on history, botany or zoology. *All* of them want to turn man into an encyclopedia at the expense of reality and life. Every educator really ought to recognize this.

While the teacher is occupied with such thoughts, a short educational treatise comes flying through the mail and into his house. Its author is not a nobody, but a professor of psychology and education and a consultant to the Ministry of Education. What does this expert on education espouse? Teaching the encyclopedia as the ultimate preparation for real life.

> The student who does not learn how to use the modern encyclopedia will be unable to meet the demands of life. . . . Teaching the encyclopedia is a valuable, even indispensable part of the ultimate preparation for real life.

The teacher is shocked by this piece of deep pedagogical insight and thinks, From all sides, from every book and every journal on education I am receiving the same message: a great common front aimed *against* the soul of the child. But the child is defenseless against the adult. Does the child then no longer have a guardian angel? It is always the same old story: The child is supposed to be deprived of the opportunity to develop as a free, self-aware human being. What is he given for this purpose? Dogma, machine and encyclopedia. Certainly, many other things serve the same end, but it always involves an unhealthy giving and taking.

As a teacher, I prefer to adhere to Troxler and Nietzsche. Nietzsche's ill-timed work "The Use and Abuse of History" contains words seldom heard that challenge our thinking and appear to point in the right direction:

> Excess of history has attacked life's plastic powers, it no longer knows how to employ the past as a nourishing food.[7]

The most powerful . . . nature . . . would draw to itself .
. . all the past and . . . transform it into blood.[8]

What could that mean for the educator? With the teacher's
help, the child should be able to absorb history in such a
way that it is absorbed by his entire organism and becomes
part of his innermost being, in such a way that he carries
within him something quite different from merely x amount
of knowledge. Thus, history should transform itself into a
life force, but it is destroying that life force instead, and
Nietzsche is forced to ask himself "how the health of a people undermined by the study of history may be again restored"[9] He, himself, can still provide the answer to this
question, namely, only by a hygiene of life.

> . . . a hygiene of life belongs close beside science and one
> of the clauses of this hygiene would read: the unhistori-
> cal and the suprahistorical are the natural antidotes to
> the stifling of life by the historical, by the malady of
> history.[10]

I feel I am tracking down the secret of the subject matter, the teacher says to himself. But the secret is connected
to a new teaching doctrine that is a hygiene of life, and not a
doctrine that teaches how self-awareness, as it appears in the
child, can best be destroyed, smothered or twisted. None of
the teaching manuals I have used up to now lead to this
hygiene of life. They all want to mislead me into giving death
with one hand and taking life with the other. All subject
matter that is derived from "historical thinking," even if it
is simplified for the child, is stone instead of bread.

What is to be done? With Silesius's verse in mind I answer,
God's eternal Word, as well as life and spirit can be found in
the subject matter. But how? My best and strongest feelings
do not seem to help me there. I get a little closer to things,

but not in a way that helps me understand them. As for my thinking, is it any different from what Nietzsche fought so much against, which cannot bring to life, but can only destroy, which is a barrier to understanding plants, animals and other people?

I have come this far with my insights: Others think either that they have grasped the nature of things when they hold only the outer husks, or they do not think about it at all any more. I know, however, that everything real escapes my grasp. Furthermore, I know that all the prescribed subject matter can be of no great value to the child's self, because it contains no living force. But what good are these nice insights? In the end, is not the illusion or even the ignorance of others better for the teacher in this day and age?

After a while our teacher adopts an increasingly negative view of his own thinking. It can only separate, it can only differentiate: Here am I and there is "it," the world.

Then he has a stroke of great good fortune. He reads Rudolf Steiner's *The Philosophy of Freedom*, and the following thoughts, among others, begin to live inside him:

> . . . In thinking, we have got hold of one corner of the whole world process which requires our presence if anything is to happen . . . Hence for the study of all that happens in the world there can be no more fundamental starting point than thinking itself . . . It must, however, not be overlooked that only with the help of thinking am I able to determine myself as subject and contrast myself with the objects. Therefore thinking must never be regarded as a merely subjective activity. Thinking lies *beyond* subject and object . . . Thinking is thus an element which leads me out beyond myself and connects me with the objects. But at the same time it separates me from them, inasmuch as it sets me, as subject, over against them. It is just this which constitutes the double nature

of man. He thinks, and thereby embraces both himself and the rest of the world. But at the same time it is by means of thinking that he determines himself as an *individual* confronting the *things.*[11]

These words solve the riddle that has plagued the teacher, and bring him the solution for which he has unconsciously been searching for so long. I am beginning to understand the nature of thinking, he may now say to himself. Thinking opened the abyss and isolated me from the world around me. The abyss was not always there and will not have to last forever. What builds the bridges over the abyss? Thinking itself. It can perform both functions. I trust thinking again. What I myself separated through one aspect of thinking is transformed into full reality by the other. The first aspect of thinking is given to me without any special effort on my part. I recognize it as self-evident. The other aspect of thinking, however, (which is the force that connects me to the world), exists in me only as a potential. I must acquire it, earn it. This new insight leads me to act; it awakens the will forces in me.

The teacher now reaches for Rudolf Steiner's book *Knowledge of the Higher Worlds and Its Attainment* in which the first sentence reads, "There slumber in every human being faculties by means of which he can acquire for himself a knowledge of the higher worlds."[12] As he tries to follow this path of knowledge, he experiences the same thing as thousands of others. He constantly stumbles over his own thought lethargy, or his thoughts run away from him and slip robot-like right back into the same old rut. Hundreds of times he trips, and hundreds of times he catches himself again. Finally, after long and hard work, he reaps the first reward: a faint inkling of what a transformation of consciousness might be.

He says to himself, This book is a path of knowledge for

the teacher; it is his exercise book. In it lie all teaching possibilities, but the teacher must draw on himself for these possibilities, not on the book. The book serves only to direct him to himself in the right way.

The teacher now knows: through these two books I can *become* a man and a teacher. Until now I believed that I *was* a man and a teacher; now I see that I must first become one. What a turnaround! What seemed a complete man has become one that is developing. I gain enormously thereby. The road has been cleared for further growth. To date I led only a phantom existence, yet it was strong enough to impede my growth. Now I know that I must give up that phantom existence if I truly wish to become a teacher. It will take a long time, and I must develop the capacity to allow something to mature slowly. In this context, nothing good can be said of finishing as quickly as possible.

But now the teacher is in for new surprises. He comes across Rudolf Steiner's lectures on education. Upon reading them a new world opens before him. First he experiences an emotion he often felt as a child: amazement. He is amazed by the incredible fullness of the new world. He is amazed by the man whose creative power of knowledge permeates the lectures. Amazement turns into awe, and this awe prevents him from simply plundering the wealth offered in these lectures. Amazement and awe turn into recognition. He recognizes that Rudolf Steiner's lectures on education are not merely random pieces of flotsam tossed up on shore by life's stormy seas. In other words, they are not there for any scavenger to sift through and pick out what just happens to appeal to him.

The teacher recognizes the nature of these writings more and more. In the end, they, too, are exercise books, he says to himself, especially for the teacher. They are not supposed to be put into practice immediately, at least not if you use them properly. Each lecture is like a new path by which the reader can awaken the proper educational force in himself. This is true not only with regard to the child, but also with regard to the subject matter. They are exercises, meditation material for the teacher. Any one of Rudolf Steiner's thoughts, if constantly rethought and practiced, turns into the force of perception, which is educational in nature. Rudolf Steiner's indications, as they are called, are a special kind of gift. If they cannot also be forgotten at a given moment, they become (through no one's fault but our own) mere stones, and thus totally worthless . . .

Let us assume that I want to teach botany and that I find the following indication, among many:

> When the earth lets mushrooms grow, it keeps the growing power of the tree inside. But when the earth lets trees grow, then it pushes the growing power of the tree to the outside.

Reading this I know that you cannot use such an indication as class material, not even if it takes up half a lecture. You might be able to fill a measly half hour of the school day that way, but to no one's benefit. (Of course, out of embarrassment and confusion, you will probably end up doing it anyway one day, even though you know better.)

If you take up such an indication in the right way, however, it can become the foundation of an entire botany class. For thus used, it is the impetus for educating the living powers of thought, which alone can open an approach to the living processes of the organic world. And lo and behold, the plant pressed between two books opens up into the vast cosmos. I feel that the same objective, living thought-world that has come to life within me also lives outside me in the organic world. The plants are its most beautiful and pure expression. Is it still true that the plant's life is a mystery to me?

If I want to teach zoology, I must try to understand the inner nature of the animal. The lectures on education are full of helpful suggestions. They are meant only as hints, however, indicating where to look for the knowledge necessary to the teacher. Everyone is on his own in following the path itself. No one else can do it for him.

The teacher might find this hint, for example:

> In the course of becoming a man I went through what is now visible to me in lions and snakes; I lived in all those forms, because my own innermost being went through the qualities developed in these animals.

As subject matter this indication is entirely useless. It may not be immediately applied simply as an "idea." It must first become alive in the teacher, thereby undergoing a total transformation. What he has brought to life in himself in this manner now allows him to teach every aspect of zoology, for the teacher now becomes aware of himself, of his soul qualities, of the "animals" in himself. Having awoken in this way, he might meet with the following adventure: He stands at his workbench, carving-knife in hand and a block of wood before him. He begins to carve the head of a noble horse out of the wood as a hobbyhorse for his son. At least, that is what he would like to do. But since he does not want to follow a set pattern and begins to carve using only his own imagination, something else comes out of the wood. What was supposed to become a horse looks increasingly like a fox! The teacher looks at his peculiar creation. It has really become a fox, with pointy snout and cunning look. An inescapable self-recognition takes place: A soul quality buried deep inside you has decided to express itself outwardly for a change. The foxy nature in you has become visible. What a lesson in self-recognition for that teacher. How often must he say to himself, Stop, now the fox in you is slyly trying to get the upper hand again! Or, Your foxlike cleverness allows you to do everything totally without commitment so that it is never you, but always someone else who suffers.

In this way, however, the teacher practices constant self-control. He becomes skeptical—of himself! He remembers Morgenstern's words: "Higher than all knowledge I place self-control, the absolute skepticism towards oneself." He recalls Nietzsche's educational insight: "The true teacher takes things seriously only as they affect the children—even himself."

Now that the teacher's will forces have been called forth by recognitions such as these, he may dare to begin teaching zoology. He can legitimately do so by virtue of his own recognition and his own will. He needs no diploma from a certifying institution or the recommendation of another individual. He is able to present animals not as stuffed hides, the way they appear in books, but as beings permeated with formative soul forces.

During his internal dialogue the teacher says to himself, I am supposed to teach the children grammar. How can I accept that responsibility when that is exactly where I can see only uniform grayness? Of course, my common sense tells me that grammar has something to do with human speech and thus with mankind itself. But other than that I feel no human connection to it. This unfruitful skepticism toward grammar is transformed into trust through the indications of Rudolf Steiner, one of which reads as follows:

> When I pronounce a noun, I separate myself from the world around me; when I pronounce an adjective, I bind myself to the world around me; and when I pronounce a verb, I am active in the world around me.

Something seems to be shining through these words. But now the teacher's work begins. It consists in using this indication to draw out clearly, colorfully and beautifully what begins to shine, in delicate colors, through the uniformly gray wall. What is it the teacher draws out? His own picture —the picture of threefold man. In this way grammar becomes a school of self-knowledge and sharpened awareness for the teacher. He also knows *what agent* has covered the many-faceted picture in shades of gray: his own intellect. For that reason he will never again say to himself: This is how the world *is*, but rather, this is how I have made the world with my intellect, which is why it now *appears* this way to me.

What prevents the teacher now from venturing to teach grammar . . .?

The teacher now recognizes in world history the story of mankind's evolving consciousness. Without this recognition world history becomes "historical" in the worst sense. An essential prerequisite to understanding world history is the experience, no matter how slight, of a transformation of consciousness. It must at least be felt what a transformation of consciousness could be. That is what Nietzsche suspected when he wrote these words:

> If you are to venture to interpret the past you can do so only out of the fullest exertion of the vigor of the present: Only when you put forth your noblest qualities in all their strength will you divine what is worth knowing and preserving in the past. Like to like! Otherwise you will draw the past down to you.[13]

That must mean, Do not risk approaching history with the usual flippancy; that way you will certainly grasp the everyday life of today, but not the thinking, feeling and willing of a bygone race. The essence of things, that which has been effective, beneath the surface, slips out of the net of your intellect. But anthroposophy leads me to recognize like through like, though not without a great deal of personal

effort. To the extent that anthroposophy helps me to overcome a merely dictionary-oriented existence, that purely
phantom life (and with it the "historical man"), I am able
to understand history. What do I get in return? I get the
"strength to create something *new* out of the foundations of
existence." It gives me, the teacher, the opportunity to give
the child history like a food for his soul forces, so that he
may digest it in his blood, muscles, even his bones. Slowly I
begin to understand words such as these:

> The development of muscles around the bones depends
> on the presence of great role models in the world. Even if
> an individual can follow these examples only in his head,
> the muscle and bone structure begins to mesh.

Rudolf Steiner once said: "The death of a science has occurred
when it no longer becomes anyone's inner experience."

As a teacher I can also interpret these words in this way:
The death of teaching can be said to have occurred when the
subject matter no longer becomes an inner experience for
the teacher. If it is to have educational impact, all of a
teacher's preparatory work must become a deeply internal
matter. It becomes a problem that must be solved through a
transformation of the teacher's consciousness. After the preparatory work, I can no longer be quite the same as before.

As long as I make no effort to transform my consciousness, I will not be able to place the subject matter in the service of education. What I can grasp through the second
aspect of my thinking, however, is no longer mere subject
matter. Reality and spiritual will are already living in it,
working into the child and unfolding his forces. The subject
matter alone, as the by-product of passive, intellectual
thinking, has a destructive and crippling effect on the child.
It makes the child ill.

Now this, the teacher may say to himself, is a new and

healing teaching method. Nietzsche's challenge was first met, sixty years later, by Rudolf Steiner. Nietzsche, the diagnostician, could not progress to a therapy, which in this case means a method. He stopped with the challenge. It is up to us, then, to become therapists instead of remaining mere teaching technicians.

Now I understand Troxler as well: Education is releasing and freeing. It neither gives nor takes. The reference to truth made by the baccalaureate in Goethe's Faust II, that "each [teacher] knows the way to lessen or exceed it [the truth]"[14], is no longer valid. For me it is no longer a case of giving to the child so that he has something, namely a necessary supply of knowledge, from which he can draw as needed later in life (whereby the soul of the child is seen as a storage room. Instead I "give" to the child, so that he can become something: a full-fledged human being, but out of his very own powers. I "give" to the child, so that something becomes alive in him. What I give to him as subject matter I give to him only as an echo of the world, as an echo, and not as exclusive and sole reality. I am not even allowed to give the child something that he may keep in that exact conceptual form. Nothing should be permanently stamped on the child's mind like a taped message, the way the recorder does it.

I also clearly recognize that education is not "primarily a process of tearing down," the way the seminar director and other newer theologies would have it, but rather a continuous healing process.

I understand Rudolf Steiner's words better and better. *The subject matter is medicinal in the hand of the teacher.*

Yet, we are dealing with something quite different here from the external chemical process used in a laboratory to produce a medicine. We are dealing with a spiritual chemistry within the teacher, with a chemical process in his soul. *Only that which has transformed itself in me through my own ef-*

forts has a healing, releasing and nourishing effect on the child.

For that reason I must not look to replace myself, the teacher, with the tape recorder. That is merely an escape, both from myself and from the inner voice saying, "Transform thyself," and is therefore nothing less than an act of true desperation by man as he is today. *I may not remove myself, but I must become transparent.* The entire world must appear to the child through me and permeate him with power. Then the child, through me his teacher, can awaken to the world and unfold his self in the right way.

I can look at it any way I like, says our fictitious teacher, whose life story now comes to a close: Teaching is nothing less than a mystery, a great wonder, even if it does not always seem that way from the outside.

Teaching Botany and Zoology

We have all been witness to a miracle: In our garden there grows a plant; with our physical eyes we see only its leaves and stem with a flower bud. This so-called flower bud, however, is still more leaf than flower, for we see only numerous little green leaves in a tight little bundle. Thus, the plant as we see it one evening is still completely "leaf." The leaves may have various shapes and sizes (when seen up close, even the stem has a certain leafiness), but leaves they are nonetheless, and therefore they appear as a uniform "green on green." Overnight, however, the plant seems to push something entirely new out of itself, and the next morning an extremely delicate and colorful blossom pokes out its head. Though this fragrant blossom bears hardly any resemblance to the leaf any more, it is still the same plant, which has simply chosen to manifest itself for a time as a moist, green leaf. Then, suddenly, it blazed forth as a brilliant flower. Consider the leap that nature appears to make here. It is entirely possible that in a single night the blossom potential—invisible the day before—will burst out in all its glory. The divine miracle is that one and the same force can manifest itself in the sense-perceptible world in so many different ways, all according to the laws of nature.

Whoever has disciplined his own powers by inwardly participating in the metamorphoses of the plant being will eventually be able to follow the metamorphoses of something much more complex than the plant, namely the human being. I am not referring to the finished human being (why should anyone be interested in a "finished being"?), but to the developing human being, above all, the child. He who has disciplined his thinking on the plant finds to his amazement that the development of the child is neither constant nor regular, and that the progression from one stage to the next is not simply a matter of causality. On the contrary, he realizes that the "being of this child" makes leaps and bounds. A child entrusted to him may undergo no major changes at all for quite some time, during which everything remains "green on green." At the end of that time, however, changes occur in rapid succession. He sees that forces become manifest whose origin is at first a mystery, and which seem to mold an almost completely new being out of the child.

There are thus certain ages that represent turning points in the child's life. The first occurs around the age of seven. The second, which though too seldom recognized is still extremely important, takes place between the ages of nine and ten. Based on my own experience, I would like to address both the changes that the child undergoes around this time and their significance for education.

If we wish to appreciate all the changes that occur in a child between the ages of nine and ten, even if we limit ourselves to what is visible from the outside, we must first be able to picture children of seven and eight. Thus, in order to clarify what comes later, I will describe—albeit very sketchily and without covering anywhere near everything—some of the things that a teacher can observe in children of this age.

How lightly a seven-year-old child still skips and flits and floats across the earth, and with what an instinctive sureness his feet "know" how to circumvent obstacles. Every second you think: Now he's going to fall, that will bring on the tears and screams, and a bloody nose on top of it. But look! Not a scratch on him! Lightly and surely he was led past the danger. (But by whom?)

Clearly, the child lives its life in rhythms. How does the child experience the world? you may ask yourself.

In order to sense his true being you need only watch again and again how before going to bed a child of that age always says goodnight to the flowers and trees in the garden, the neighbor's chickens and dog, and the clouds in the sky. Or tell him a fairy tale. Then you begin to suspect what kind of "nourishment" the true being of a child must receive every day. Without this nourishment he will be stunted and gnawed on by so-called real life, the life of adults, which, like a hungry dragon, is all too ready to devour the true being of the child.

Before the age of nine, a child—and I mean a relatively unspoiled child—really makes no distinction at all between himself and the world. He experiences the world directly, because until now no barrier stands between them. Inwardly, he can become one with the world at any time. Therefore hardly anything is "dead" for such a child; everything is alive to him, just as he experiences his own life. His actions are determined by the overriding strength of his sympathies for things.

The adult as educator is somehow a natural authority for him and for that reason alone is worth imitating. The child at this age does not yet have a sharp eye for the weaknesses of adults. If we wanted to verbalize his unconscious attitude towards adults, it might go something like this: I know I am often naughty, wild, unruly and bad-mannered. You, Mr. Adult, must put up with a lot from me. But it would never occur to me not to acknowledge you as absolute authority.

What this implies for education is obvious to see, if very difficult to put into practice. The teacher better make sure that he becomes worth imitating; that his uncontested position of authority works to the advantage of the child. He must be so full of life that he can offer the child a picture of the world in which nothing is "dead." He must be able to give his imagination free rein, and to speak of plants and animals, clouds and mountains in such a way that the child sees them as living beings. At the same time, he must be sure that in speaking to the children in this way he does not use baby talk, but, on the contrary, a language that is wiser and at least as concrete and real as that of science. His teaching, therefore, has a certain unity, and there is no clear-cut division of subjects. At this age children are found to be extremely eager for knowledge, but they want to grasp everything with their feelings and as a picture. Everything that cannot be grasped in this way they skip over, unless they are forced by sharp, external pressure to do the opposite of what is natural and healthy for them.

The children live in this environment until they turn nine, when their nature takes a mighty leap. The changes that now come to light can be particularly striking to the teacher when, after a long vacation, he once again has the children before him in the classroom or watches them running around the playground. Then he notices, for example, that the children are rather less coordinated than before, that the instinctive surefootedness is no longer there. Instead of the often light, dancing steps their tread is now somehow heavier. Also, they no longer abandon themselves so totally to rhythm. In a song, rhythm is no longer of equal or even greater importance than the melody. Now it is clearly the latter to which the child listens and relates. He is no longer at all pleased, for example, when the teacher claps the rhythm of a song or poem with his hands in order to emphasize the beat.

The relationship to the teacher changes altogether. To

his dismay, the teacher might suddenly become aware that he is standing *opposite* his children, and that a dangerous chasm has opened between him and them that was not there before. The children have slipped away from me during the vacation, he may say to himself, and he feels wistful, or even uncomfortable, for the children are looking at him with more probing, more critical eyes.

A small, and in itself completely trivial event reveals to the teacher the new situation in which he finds himself. Wiping the blackboard during a lesson the eraser slips out of his hands and hops to the floor. Now, this had happened to him once before, and what was the reaction then? The children, delighted by the unexpected game, threw themselves on the eraser, each one wanting to catch it first and bring it to the teacher. This created a cheerful mood in the children that lingered on for the remainder of the lesson. Without a doubt, the unspoken opinion among the children was that the teacher had dropped the eraser for their very special amusement. And now, one year later? One child does, in fact, bring the eraser back, but somehow the children's faces reveal their astonishment that their teacher could be so clumsy.

Another symptom: The teacher walks down the street with his children. Not very long ago he had far too few hands at such times for all the children hanging on him. Now he has exactly two hands too many. He senses that a slight alienation has occurred between himself and the children. Their relationship to him, though unnoticeable to the insensitive observer, is strained. Why the sudden reserve?

Nevertheless, the children continue to ask many questions. Now, however, they are asked out of a different inner situation. Before, questions were asked out of a desire to chatter and yell and tell stories, as though it did not matter what the teacher answered as long as he was prepared to listen patiently and alertly. Now, the questions are more careful and more urgent, and infinitely more depends on the answers than before. It is at this age that the questions about the beginning and end of the world crop up again as they did after the children turned seven, but this time they are no longer satisfied with the same answers. What came before God and the holy spirits, they may actually ask you. Or a child might ask, You can't think anymore if your heart is cut out, right? And they are suddenly capable of the most over-precise answers! A father says to his nine-and-a-half-year-old child at the table, "That was extremely rude of you. It does not become you at all." The child answers, "That's just the way I am now. God must have wanted me to be like this or he would have created me differently."

At this age the child becomes aware that there are varying social conditions and class differences. (If he spoke of it before, it was somehow unnatural, and the fault of adults.) "Daddy, are we rich or poor?" the children often ask in this stage of development. They notice how important money is for adults, and that begins to preoccupy them a great deal. They look for standards against which they can measure the world. They strive mightily to understand the world, but above all they would now like to see through and through adults. "Daddy," asks a child, "why did you leave B____ and move to Basel, anyway? Do you earn more money here?" The father sees through the child who wants to see through the adult and answers, "No, I earn less money here than I did there." The child, however, wants to solve this puzzle at all costs and asks, "But then why did you move to Basel?" The father answers, "Because I enjoy my work here more than I did there." The child notices: Here is a mystery I have not tracked down yet, and in front of me stands an adult whom I do not yet fully see through. For days afterwards the child asks his father the trickiest questions about this impenetrable mystery in order to understand what still lies outside his understanding. It is good, however, if the child does not completely see through the adult, if he feels that the adult has something in him which he, the child, can come to understand only gradually.

Children of this age often have very frightening dreams, a sign of how powerfully daytime experiences stay with them.

Such a child may suddenly give his mother quite a shock by saying, "You know, Mommy, none of the fairy tales are true; and as for angels, they don't exist at all." He says it with the tone, gesture and above all with the conviction of an atheist itinerant preacher. But when the child lies in bed at night he wants his mother to tell him a fairy tale and cannot fall asleep without it. And how does he listen? With enormous interest. He lives in the reality of the fairy tale himself, and as a result he recites the prayer of the fourteen angels with even greater fervor than before.

What a strange, dual being we have before us. Something in him says there are no angels, particularly no gnomes and elves and giants. With the rest of his being, however, he still lives in the world beyond the senses in the most natural way, and there he seeks nourishment for his soul. Does it not seem that such a child could perceive the world with a dual consciousness and therefore in two different ways? On what could such a duality be based?

In his educational books and lectures Rudolf Steiner frequently called particular attention to this developmental stage in the child. It is, therefore, understandable if the teacher, having read such material, devotes special attention to children between nine and ten and follows their further development with keener awareness. It then becomes steadily clearer to him that something extremely significant is happening in the child's being, namely a true change of consciousness.

After the age of nine, a child truly does step out of his previous state of consciousness in order to perceive the world in a new way. We adults can at first only experience the world by making a sharp distinction between ourselves as subject and the world as object. We easily make the mistake of concluding that the small child forms the same (if "cruder," "dumber," etc.) relationship to the world that we do.

Had we been instilled with better powers of observation, however—even adults can still learn new tricks—then we would have had to see in the way a seven- or eight-year-old child behaves towards a flower, animal or any object, that the child is nowhere near ready to make this sharp distinction. On the contrary, we would not overlook how the child loses itself inwardly in that object, that a common soul cloud still envelops both the child and the object that happens to catch his attention. For this reason it is impossible for the child to make the conscious distinction between himself and the environment as two different things the way the adult does.

After the ninth year, however, the image-creating soul cloud, which protectively envelops the child and his world, fades away. The child sees "more clearly" now. He sees himself suddenly standing opposite things and feels forced to keep his distance from them. They become more foreign to him and, therefore, questionable. The entire world, in which he so recently participated without effort, somehow becomes questionable and full of riddles. Hence all the questions asked by children, which are often less important for their content than for the inner tension that caused them to be asked.

That is why the child at this stage loves and hungers for riddles, lots of riddles. I know a father who had to tell his nine-and-a-half-year-old child riddles every single morning on the way to school. At first he was annoyed, but in the end he was able, sometimes more successfully than others, to present everything in the child's immediate environment as a riddle: trees and animals, houses and telephone poles, sun and stars. It did the child a visible good each time he was smart enough to solve the riddle. He had now grasped the being or object that had been clothed in such a riddle by means of his *own* reasoning powers.

The reverse is also true. How unsettled and "nervous" children become when they just cannot solve the riddle. The object then seems to become a threatening monster for them because they were unable to guess its identity.

Why, we may ask, can the child now distinguish between himself and the environment? Because something inside him has separated itself from the psychic foundation. Let us immediately put a name to what has separated itself: the intellectual forces. The child's first very own powers of understanding make their appearance; the first intellectual capacity for differentiation is born. *This* force makes the child critical when it comes to the adult (how "arrogant" and "impertinent" children can be at this age!) and simultaneously alienates him from the environment. This is why he no longer feels at one with the world in the same natural way. Inwardly, he begins to freeze. He feels himself kicked out of Paradise. You cannot help thinking about the story of Paradise when you go through this stage of development with children. In an old Paradise play Adam says after having eaten the apple:

> Oh, how my soul has changed . . .
> I am quite naked and unprotected.

A second picture can be evoked when dealing with children of this age. As the intellectual forces rise "up" out of the undifferentiated realm of the soul, the will forces are undergoing a change at the other end of the spectrum and demand immediate and proper reinforcement.

The teacher is thus presented with a situation in which a very complex being stands before him, whose own complexity unconsciously pains him. The teacher must now instruct and educate that being.

It is easy to see that children of this age present the teacher with a special challenge. Turning that nice-sounding insight into proper educational action, however, is very difficult. On one level, the child has become equal to the adult. Consequently, the child can no longer accept that adult as unquestioned authority as he did before. Yet, it is precisely at this critical moment that the child needs a leader and helper more than ever. The teacher is thus faced with the task of rebuilding his authority on a new foundation. What sufficed until now will no longer do. How does he go about doing this? According to Rudolf Steiner, "the teacher must now grow beyond himself." In other words, in order to continue growing the teacher must be able to leave behind that level on which the child has become his equal.

How easy it is for the teacher to lose the trust of the children at this point. Haven't we all lost every child's trust at some time or another? The teacher must regain it every day, or at least try to regain it.

There is a second question we must ask our conscience: Have we always given the correct answer to all of a child's questions? Who of us has such a fine ear that we can also hear and answer the child's unexpressed questions, whether in private conversation or in class?

Where is the cloak with which to cover our weaknesses and shortcomings so that they cannot be uncovered by the probing stare of a ten-year-old?

Everything now depends on whether the teacher can still educate himself. This then determines the degree to which he can make today's problematic world understandable to the children in his class, and the degree to which he succeeds in using the individual subjects to reach the child in all his complexity and to strengthen his soul forces.

Of course, the eight- and nine-year-old child is hungry for knowledge of the world, too, but he can absorb that knowledge only as something whole, as a myth, fairy tale or fable, that is, in the form of pictures saturated with life. Be it tree or stream, moss or stone, all are living beings that can speak to the child as well as to their own kind. For such a child, if he is not completely spoiled by adults yet, it is quite normal for the teacher to speak about these things indiscriminately as living beings. In fact, it is what he craves deep down inside. The teacher is therefore faced with the "challenge" of grasping the living processes of nature with his own soul forces in such a way that he can raise them into images. These images strengthen the spiritual in the child, provided they are not contrived or created by an overactive imagination, but express a reality. The heart forces are thereby developed in a healthy way.

On the other hand, if you are involved with children in their tenth year, it is clear—this is after all a truism—that the teacher must now present the world he wants to bring into the classroom in a much more sophisticated way than before. The beings must be distinctly separated. An animal is something quite different from a plant, not to mention a mountain. Every object has its own character about which the child would like to learn. What until now lived unseparated in the lap of a living and ancient oneness separates in the classroom into the various subjects such as botany, zoology, geography, etc. . . .

Upon closer observation, these subjects prove by their very complexity to be the most valuable tools in bringing the likewise complex soul forces of the children to a healthy unfolding: the heart forces, the newborn intellectual thinking forces and the restrained will forces that no longer want to express themselves only through the limbs.

Admittedly, a quite different attitude towards the teaching material than currently accepted arises out of the new perspective. It turns out that in its true nature the teaching material is by no means an end in itself. It does not exist simply to be memorized by the teacher as mere material, only to be unloaded on the children unchanged, if "simplified" and in smaller doses. It is only the means to an end. The end of teaching, however, is education—meaning the most powerful development possible of *all* the human forces. The teaching material becomes a real means of education only if the teacher recognizes that this "material" (allow me to use the word material literally here) is woven by divine hands. This demonstrates that all education is first and foremost a problem of consciousness for anyone who wants to teach. What the teacher wants to bring to the child from the world must first have become an inner experience for him. After the proper preparation, the teacher is no longer the same as he was before, but this change has nothing to do with a greater or lesser amount of knowledge.

This attitude is certainly not a forgone conclusion for today's civilized man. Without it, however, you will not be able to teach, but at most instruct. The teacher who does not adopt this attitude may become a highly sophisticated teaching technician, but, in the words of Nietzsche, he then serves the "coming barbarism." The present situation, however, demands something quite different from the teacher: Rather than letting himself turn into a teaching technician, he should teach himself to be a therapist.

Only to the extent that he is successful in this will he be able to strengthen the thinking, feeling and willing of his children in a healthy way. What happens to the children otherwise? Their mental capacity dries up, becomes steadily more narrow and biting and, cut off from all reality, loses all fruitfulness. The result is either rigid thinking, which will collapse before every difficult situation, or an absence of thinking power altogether, rendering the individual incapable of recognizing even the tasks and problems at hand. The will forces, on the other hand, are either weakened or derailed, becoming steadily more wild, rebellious and compulsive. The feeling life, however, can dwindle to the point of almost total coarseness, unless the individual escapes into sentimentality (the surrogate for healthy feeling).

Some of you may contend that although too little has been "done" for the feeling and will forces until now, the education of the intellect has not been neglected. My question is, With what result? A small example may shed some light on an already well-known fact. A man with a fairly important position in the business world enrolls his son in my class. In the course of a conversation he says to me that he is less than anxious for his son to acquire great learning and knowledge. When I express my dismay he explains that his main concern is for his child to maintain a certain freshness in his thinking and, moreover, that it is precisely in school that this fresh, quick thinking is ruined. In his dealings with trainees and employees he claims to have observed this phenomenon very clearly. The less formal education a young person has received, the more able, sensibly and intelligently he will perform on the job. Why? Because he still has a certain store of healthy common sense, especially if he has only attended an elementary school. But the more education young people have (especially those with a high school diploma), the more they approach a job without ideas or thoughts.

This example, as crude as it may seem, reveals a special tragedy. Starting with the first year of school, even with the first day, education is directed towards the child's thinking, attempting year after year to develop it more intensely. The peculiar result is that complaints come in from all quarters (not only from businessmen) that the graduates are scatter-brained and unable to think even halfway sequentially.

Could it be that we want to do too much in school, in the wrong way and, above all, at the wrong time? Before what we hope to develop in the child has naturally matured to a stage that can be further developed in a legitimate way? In any educational action, what matters is not *that* something is done, but *how* it is done and *when*.

I am going to whittle the multitude of questions that arise here down to one single question: Do subjects exist that develop living thinking and a will strongly connected to human dignity?

I have already mentioned Rudolf Steiner's lectures on education. They represent neither recipes nor an educational system. They act as stimulators, as signposts. (Go in this direction if you want to find what you are seeking.) They always point to the *path* that should be taken. The same is true of Rudolf Steiner's teaching plan, which is the result of a true psychology. The teacher finds valuable help there, especially if his educational forces have just been born and are thus still extremely delicate and weak. He might read these words: "It is good to begin with zoology and botany in the fourth grade." Out of a certain trust, which previous experiences seem to justify, he does just that, very curious about the new experiences he will have.

The *what* is thus given, but now comes the *how*. *How* should these two worlds in nature be taught as subjects? The answer can only be: according to their true, living nature. If the teacher is successful—after a lot of hard work—then these two subjects prove to be important tools in teaching children between nine and ten. He now understands their fundamentally different educational effect on the child and knows how to use them to that end.

Let us thus try to find the path leading to the special nature of plants, and please excuse my rather elementary approach. Imagine we go outdoors one day in March. The sun is shining, and we contentedly feel its mild rays warm our back. The streets are already lightly dusted with pollen. In defiance of the mild sunshine, however, a biting wind is still glowing, and standing in the shade we begin to freeze. The Jura mountains are still tipped with snow and the ground in the valley, though thawed, is still cold and damp. We now turn off the main street onto a track across the fields and come to a quarry. There, where a mound of broken-up earth absorbs the sun's rays, we see something wonderful: A thick little stalk is growing out of the ground, surrounded by dozens of thick greenish-brown leaves, and all of these have a soft, furry texture. At the top, however, the little stalk turns into a small sunburst of golden petals. Where I live we call these March flowers, but they are also called coltsfoot. As we observe this little plant—how it grows out of *this* soil, in *this* biting air, towards *this* mild March sun and offers it its flower—we may come to the sudden realization that we can understand this plant only by turning our gaze to the sun, to that which works on the earth from the heavens, and to the earth, to the special composition of the soil at this time of year.

Now, let the seasons pass from Spring through Summer to Fall. One Fall afternoon we take a walk in the fields. The trees are already throwing long shadows across the meadows. We walk across the meadow grass. A little brook coming out of the nearby forest waters the ground. And now we see a flower of the most delicate purple shimmering through the still lush, green grass. Of leaves we see nothing. Out of the dark earth grows something pale and stem-like, which turns more and more into the slender flower petals. It is the meadow saffron.

If we now clear our minds of all external learning and book knowledge, silence everything that may be preoccupying us and give ourselves in inner silence, but in full awareness, at least momentarily to the phenomena as presented to us here, then we will again experience that this plant can only be understood as the beautiful, tangible image of a very specific relationship between heaven and earth.

The path of the sun and all the heavenly bodies is reflected in all plants that grow, bloom and winter in a continuous cycle between Spring and Fall. This path is modified by the surface of the earth and all the rest of the earthly environment. In the plant we see two polar forces at work, heaven and earth, and the plant is the living expression of their interplay.

Only in this way do we approach the true nature of the plant. The plant belongs to the heavens and the earth, and must never be separated from these two in our observation. Therefore, the plant that has been ripped from the earth, purely as an object of observation, is nothing but a lie. We approach the reality of the plant only if we look at it as a tangible image of earthly and heavenly activity. Here is the earth (sandy, clayey, moist, dry), there is the sun, moon and stars. Each *new* plant, *each* new vegetation is the visible expression of the fact that something in that interplay has changed. The plants are the faithful reflection of all these changes. It is important that the children follow these changes and transformations with their first intellectual forces, that they be allowed to experience the plants as children of the earth mother and the heavenly father, that they themselves be able to express this participation of their thinking in all transformations in their own childish words. For example: The earth has a broad back, and out of it grow the herbs and the flowers, the bushes and the trees. The sun sends its rays down on the earth. They pull the plants out of the soil. At night, however, the moon glows and the stars twinkle down on the earth. The earth and the heavens create the plants. They have mighty helpers—the water and the air. The forces of the earth create the roots of the plant. Water and air help form the airy stem and the lush leaves. At the very top the stem spreads out into the calyx. The sun's light and heat rays kindle a yellow or red or blue or multicolored flower in the calyx. The flowering plant is a child of the sun.

We can also observe the "parts" of the individual plant only by searching for the forces of heaven and earth, together with their mighty helpers water and air. One and the same supersensory plant or, as Goethe would say, archetypal plant, is visible first as root, then as stem or leaf, then as flower, depending on which forces are at work on it. The archetypal plant appears as a living, objective thought being, which becomes outwardly visible in constantly changing forms depending on the relationship between heaven and earth. To what do the plants bear witness? To the workings of a *suprahuman* thought world.

What does this kind of teaching do to the child? It leads him to an objective, creative thought world. Since the child experiences the plant as arising out of the entire landscape, he approaches the external world in the right way. He must look away from himself to the earth, then to what is over the earth, namely the heavenly bodies, and finally to what moves between heaven and earth, the clouds and the wind. He becomes aware that an individual structured plant or an entire carpet of flowers both reflect the work of suprahuman forces. He experiences the object in a sensory way appropriate to his stage of development.

But how can we humans grasp the essence of this objective, formative world? Only with a faculty that is just as objective. Is it feeling? No, for that stems too much from what is subjective in man, nor can it possibly be the will forces, for these are the most personal expression of a single and unique individual. Objectivity, or at least the potential for objectivity, belongs exclusively to our thinking.

Tracing the transformations of the archetypal plant develops the objective faculty of thinking. The thinking of children is trained on the plant. On it they can form their thoughts. The plant, however, is not a dead object, but the expression of a very real, living and creative world. From this life, which lives and creates outside of him, the child develops his own living concepts and ideas. The thoughts that the child develops by following the metamorphoses of the plant are capable of growth and are alive enough to be as creative as the archetypal plant itself.

Between the ages of nine and ten the child's need for causality comes strongly into play for the first time. Botany satisfies this need in the most natural and healthy way. We may, for example, draw the children's attention to the soil. Here is dry soil, there is moist soil. Here is a shady slope, there is the sunny slope. We now let them see for themselves how the vegetation is different in each place. They then experience cause and effect quite intensely, not yet as a sterile, lifeless concept, but as a beautiful picture. In the organic world there simply is no dead causality like, for instance, in the machine.

This is an excellent opportunity to develop living thinking and true intelligence in the child through an approach to botany that corresponds to the nature of the plant. It is almost always overlooked in today's schools, usually to the detriment of the children.

But what is the path that leads to the recognition of the special nature of an animal, of a wolf, a snake, or a cow? A simple, but perhaps more accurate observation than usual can give us our first hint. We tell the children a story in which *flowers* appear, speaking and acting as living beings. Then later we tell them another story in which *animals* act and speak in the same way (as much as possible, anyway). We can then observe that the children act differently when listening to the second story than to the first, and an even greater contrast can be seen when we watch the aftereffects of these two stories. The first story somehow has a quieting, soothing effect. The second story, however, contains a force that heads straight for the innermost being of the child, grabbing and activating it. The children "identify" with the animal they have pictured in their imagination; in that moment they are the animal, and we adults say somewhat inaccurately that the children are imitating the animal. We notice that when animals are under discussion, the perception of the animal does not go from the child's feeling life up to his thinking, but rather shoots downwards into the will. I knew a melancholic child whose favorite activity was to be a sick or even dying horse. To act this out he would lie down in a wagon, stick all four limbs in the air and neigh pitifully. It was a drawn-out, plaintive cry. The child was eventually able cleverly to prolong his death as a horse for half an hour, ending it all with a last feeble whisper. This little boy had a brother of almost the same age who was a young choleric with curly red hair. When he was angry, he curled his tongue backwards so that the underside of the tongue with the blue veins was visible. While his brother was dying slowly but surely as the horse, he ran around the wagon as a wild bull that wanted to impale the whole world on its horns.

I mention this little story only to illustrate the very special relationship children have to animals. Once we become aware of this, however, we adults can also have many experiences such as the one above, all of which serve to reconfirm this relationship. What follows are two rather simple examples. Imagine we have worked ourselves up into a proper rage about something, and then happen to catch a glimpse of ourselves in a mirror. What do we see looking out at us? An ill-tempered rooster! Naturally, we have not grown wings, and we still have our two arms. Nevertheless, we have managed to turn into a rooster. Or, we meet a man (it can just as easily be a woman) on the street with a dog. We look at both of them and it suddenly dawns on us that this person is leading his own caricature around on a leash. We experience first as harmless insight that the "animal" can step out from inside a person and become visible; under certain circumstances we may see an animal as the caricature, or the completely one-sided image, of that person. Thus, we discover the secret relationship of our own deeper being to the animals. We also see it in other people, in their outer form, movement, gait, voice, and judge their deeds accordingly. We say things about other people such as: Watch out for him, he's sly as a fox; he triumphed with the courage of a lion; a bit of a butterfly, can't be relied on; he wriggles out of trouble like a snake; he's a wolf with the ladies. All these expressions are judgments in picture form. They judge whether the behavior of another human being appears moral or immoral. Behind the picture, however, lives the reality. These judgments make their way down into the curse words (you bitch, you pig, you ass), which for obvious reasons no longer have an educational effect.

Already we see quite clearly now that while plants can appear to us as the tangible images of suprahuman (cosmic-earthly) forces, the animals are the tangible images of human soul qualities. Inner experiences of one kind or another can lead us to see the "animalness" in our own being. When an earlier race of men wanted to speak of such experiences in picture form, what was the result? The fables. They are portrayals of specific soul experiences. What are the cruel tiger, the dumb monkey, the stubborn mule, the magnanimous lion, but real, concrete soul faculties in animal form, which today, in abstractions far removed from life, we call gentleness, patience and brutality? These soul experiences are the basis of the strong, educational effect of fables. They work on man's will forces, whereas some lesson or other on virtue that speaks of gentleness, patience and brutality will be entirely ineffectual in engaging the will of the child.

The educational significance of fables, especially for children under nine, must be acknowledged. Their message is that every soul quality, when subjected to inner observation, can appear as a specific animal. The entire animal kingdom lies within one and the same human being as soul capacity. The fable "teaches" us how these forces can be brought into internal harmony; how bravery and wisdom can balance each other out, etc. In that way man rises above the animal kingdom. However, he would not be able to exercise this self-educating, harmonizing activity at all if he did not possess a force that among all earthly beings he alone possesses: the *I*. The fables appeal to the will and the *I* of man through his feelings.

From here we can discover the transition to actual zoology. From here we can also understand and rely on Rudolf Steiner's words on the nature of animals. He said, for example, that "animals came into existence when human passions hardened, when they became solid and rigid."

The step from fable to zoology is nothing but a step from image to form. Now we are no longer dealing with images envisioned within, but with the outer form of animals. (The transition from painting to sculpting.) Form, however, is merely the physical expression of soul forces. If we want to understand the animal's form and thus the animal itself, we must first look at the human form, at his round head, his narrow trunk and his straight, radial limbs. It is when we start with the structure of our own body that we begin to understand the animal forms. We see the fact to which first Goethe, then his disciples, and finally Paul Vital Troxler drew our attention, each in his own way, namely that every animal has outwardly developed to perfection one of the three organic systems mentioned above, but very one-sidedly and often at the expense of the others, and that any accurate observation of nature must lead us to speak of head-animals, trunk-animals and limb-animals. It then also becomes clear that we must consider the so-called higher animals as limb-animals and (contrary to what we are apt to believe if we do not allow the pure phenomenon to speak to us) that in the lower animals (the crustaceans) we are faced with the head-animals. I have not made it my task here (tempting as it may be) to develop a detailed study of zoology according to the nature of animals. It was simply my intent to make the teacher aware of the path that can lead to such a study.

If, however, we want to understand the educational value of such an approach to zoology, it is necessary to return from the world of animals as a whole to the single human being. In himself, man has harmoniously combined the three organic systems of head, trunk and limbs (each of which is not merely a "part," but precisely a system.) But is there something else that makes him fundamentally different from, and raises him above, the animal? Yes, he has arms. (Rudolf Steiner emphasized this fact.) Man has freed the two front limbs so that they no longer serve the body's urgent needs like all four of the animal's limbs (forcing the latter's body down into an unfree, horizontal posture.) These free arms and hands are the most beautiful expression of the purely human. They are the result of an incomparable liberating act. This can become particularly impressive when watching a eurythmy performance.

What can I do with my hands? I can build an organ, play a violin, erect a cathedral, knit socks, forge a plow. All human works are created with the hands. When we ask what is specifically human, our attention is drawn to our hands. The hands want to do something, create something, perhaps something that has never been seen in that form before. The hands are the tangible image of man's free will.

Man's humanity finds its second, already weakened expression in speech. Animals can utter only sounds, every species in its own way. Man, however, speaks. The amount of animal noises mixed in with his speech depends on the extent to which he has reached his humanity—and who can claim to have reached it fully? Some people squeak more than they speak. Others have a very soft barking, growling, hissing, bleating, buzzing or quacking sound audible in their speech. Speaking does not involve the will as much as activity with the hands does.

Thinking, however, which also differentiates man from the animal, is an activity invisible from the outside.

It is important that the child realizes through his feelings that every animal has developed some part of man particularly well, and is therefore a part of him. There is something each animal can do better than man (climb, swim, fly, dig, run, weave). One sense organ is better developed.

To such a magnificent head as the octopus man cannot lay claim. As supple a spine as the snake is impossible for him, let alone the dainty legs of a deer.

Man is the synthesis of worm, fish, lion, eagle and cow, which is why he stands *above* the animals. The force, however, that produces such a synthesis is the same force that allows man to call himself *I*. We may, therefore, call this the *I*-force.

The therapeutic effect of such teaching on the child is obvious. He feels his relationship to the animal. He sees himself, as a single individual, reflected in the animal kingdom. He experiences animalness as the image of his own form and his own soul forces. He sees himself in the animal —in the good sense and the bad. He sees where the one-sidedness of man could lead. He practices self-knowledge, albeit not yet fully consciously, in a manner corresponding to his capability and deeper yearning.

But he also sees himself raised above the animal kingdom by hands, speech and thought, and he feels the *I*-force at work in them. The alert teacher then feels the truth in words such as the following:

> The child becomes inwardly strong in his will if in this way and out of his own knowledge he sees himself grown out of the joining of all the animal elements through the living spirit that brings about this synthesis. (Rudolf Steiner)

By apprehending the nature of animals the child's will forces, which stem from his innermost subjective being, are strengthened.

The child's objective, living thinking forces are schooled by apprehending the nature of plants.

Zoology and botany give the children between nine and ten exactly what they will need later in order to realize fully the humanity which now lies dormant in them as a potential.

Teaching Grammar

Through anthroposophy we learn how to awaken to the world's phenomena. We gradually come to a realization that is especially beautiful and educationally productive: All things have meaning and exist in the world in living connection to one another. The primal spiritual source from which they stem becomes visible.

In our present natural state of awareness, however, we see these things as isolated; the living whole, of which they are only one specific expression, has vanished from our sight; the true meaning of things is hidden to us. Why do we see the world today primarily in this and no other fashion? Because a force is active in us that we call the intellect. It has isolated individual things, making each one seem to exist for its own sake, unconnected to the others, unconnected to the whole.

Seeing through this fact is of paramount importance. If we saw through it, then we could no longer say, that's how it *is*, that's how things *are*. We would have to say, I, myself, have made the world into what I see today, that is why it now looks this way to me.

Take the following, purely hypothetical situation: A great artist paints a masterpiece unparalleled for living color and form. Throughout the ages people greatly admire this wondrous painting, and they cannot gaze at its rich perfection without renewed astonishment. But then along comes a man and paints over the picture with a grayish color. This procedure is then repeated by a second man, a third man and so on. In due course the entire layer becomes thicker and thicker until finally the painting is totally obscured.

Now people come and say, Everything really *is* solid gray; who would dare deny it? How childish it was of our ancestors to claim that this painting was once alight with the purest colors and abounded with the most varied and living forms! This talk lasts just as long as it takes for someone to come and remove the many gray layers, one after the other. Then the painting begins to glow again. People say, Oh, how beautiful it is! But it was we, ourselves, who gave the painting that gray color, that's why it had to appear gray to us. Actually, however, it looks completely different.

Grammar is no different from the hypothetical situation described above. Grammar has been more or less isolated through our own doing; it has been torn from the living source. It appears to be solid gray. But when we are capable of removing the gray layers, what shines forth in bright colors to meet us? The image of man!

The study of grammar leads us (the teachers first) to our own being. It is a path to self-knowledge. But everything of value for the adult's self-education is also of value for the education of children. Then grammar no longer exists only for the intellect to practice mental gymnastics on. No, it is on the contrary an educational tool for seizing and strengthening the whole person, the willing, feeling and thinking human being.

Through grammar we can become aware of this three-fold man as revealed by a true anthropology, which is also Anthroposophy.

Rudolf Steiner calls grammar language lifted into consciousness. Grammar, after all, leads us to the essence of language; this is what we must get close to. We already get close to it when we observe how a small child learns to speak. The teacher should actually surround himself with very small children all the time, for what he learns through them can be extremely important in his teaching of older children.

How fundamentally different the manner in which a small child learns is from that of older children. What does the small child "learn" first? Not how to speak, but how to stand up, to walk, to use his arms and legs, his little feet and hands. He orients himself in space. This is the very first, most difficult, most important thing the child still has to learn. It is the foundation for everything else. On this physical and spiritual foundation speaking, too, then develops.

Thus, the child assimilates language with the creative and formative forces in his organs and weaves it into his entire organism. These are still organic forces and not yet the forces that have become intellectual, detached from the body. They reach out for the mother tongue, seize it, pull it into the depths of the organism, and there develop the organs themselves according to the power that lives in that language.

Thus, a child assimilates the language consciously by uniting his entire being with it. Even external observation shows that the thinking forces awaken only *after* the child has learned to speak. By virtue of his drive to imitate—the outward manifestation of the force in the organs—the child is able to absorb the wonderful framework of a human language as something corresponding to his being. He does not retain language in his head by means of his consciousness. Instead, the language is deeply and inseparably connected with his entire being.

What has the child pulled into his body along with language? When we examine the framework of a language as people still capable of wonder, then it can be a constant source of new miracles for us. We sense that no human intellect has worked on the structure and form of a language, but a force much wiser and more logical than the greatest wisdom and logic of a single individual. In this context Rudolf Steiner speaks of the *genius of a language*. This is not merely an allegory, or the result of an addition, or the product of individual human intellectual forces, but must be considered a real, essential force. By unconsciously using the forces working in the depths of his being to learn how to speak, the child has become one with the genius of the language itself. If the child has learned in the right way to orient himself in space through his limbs, then the sound physical foundation is present for the genius of the language to use.

When children enter school at the age of seven, they already speak fluently, although some more quickly than others. With some children the words just come bubbling out of their little mouths as though the body had lost its grip on the reins. With others the words have trouble tearing themselves out of the ground in which they are embedded. The speech of all children, however, is purely a matter of habit, and is not accompanied by full consciousness, let alone self-consciousness. When Rudolf Steiner said that teaching grammar means leading people from consciousness to self-consciousness, he voiced the educational value of grammar. Teaching grammar means making the working of the language's genius a conscious experience. But since the child has assimilated language with the forces that work on the organs rather than with his thinking forces, grammar is founded in the being of the entire person.

What follows is an excerpt from a grammar class covering the parts of speech. As we all know, orthodox grammar identifies eight or nine types of words. Three of these are quite properly accorded special importance: the verb, the adjective and the noun. The usual procedure is to introduce the child first to the nouns, then to the qualifiers and finally to the action words. But if you do not want to stand your grammar class on its head, you will begin with the action word. Watch how the small child perceives the world. His relationship to his environment consists in action, in imitative gestures; he learns his native language by speaking it. Moving his limbs is an integral part of his constitution. His "learning" is a continual effort to master something he wants to do. What he has learned is not knowledge, but immediate capability. Expressed grammatically, his relationship to the world is not substantival, but verbal.

The English teacher must take this fact into account during grammar lessons. By beginning with the verb, then moving to the adjective and ending with the noun he gives the child a conscious image of (the child's) own natural development which leads from the limbs up to the head, from concrete action to the rational establishment of an object in the world.

Accordingly, the verb quite legitimately becomes the first aspect of grammar to be taught. There is, however, something else the teacher should keep in mind, and that is that every human action is based on the will. It is always true to say that the action word expresses the will in man and thereby the realm of good and evil. Beneath every human action lies both the moral and the immoral. Man can do good or evil. Children of eight or nine, let's say, are already fairly aware of this fact, which is why they are so eager to hear stories in which beings either perform good deeds or go around making trouble. However, none of the well-meaning admonitions by adults (You must do this! You may not do that!) mean anything to them. Through the verb the child lives in active doing, in creating.

For me it was thus a question of pulling my grammar instruction out of the limbs of the children, so to speak, and bringing it into their awareness.

Now I will briefly discuss how I structured my first grammar class. The reader will have no trouble filling in the gaps properly. This is more or less what I told the children, or what I let them tell me: Each of you has two arms and two legs, two feet and two hands. Stretch your arms way out, as far away from your body as you can. Through all kinds of exercises and mutual handholding, I tried to make the children aware (by no means for the first time, I might add) that they had arms, hands and fingers with which they could do all sorts of things. It was not difficult to pick up where we had left off before. I said, for example, You already know quite well how you can use your arms with their hands and skillful fingers. The children could have gone on forever listing the things they could do with their hands. I had to bring order to this chaos of activity. Now think hard and tell me how you can use your hands to help your mother and father around the house. Again the list was long. The children themselves lived in a distinct will element. This was revealed, for example, by the fact that none of them had remained quietly seated. They had long since jumped up and waved their arms about. It had become quite clear to all of them that their hands were to help mother and father and all other people. We also spoke about what everyone could do with his hands in school, and we were amazed how different this type of handwork was from that done at home. In school it was much less a matter of lending a helping hand than of creating something beautiful for other people to enjoy.

But you have two legs as well, you say? What are they good for? Well, they all knew that they used their legs to walk to school, to jump around during recess, to take walks and to go shopping, but again we were amazed; we had hardly been able to list all the things that the hands could do, but what the legs could do was soon exhausted. They just walk around, taking our body along in the process. They are faithful servants of the body, and that is all. But this seemed a bit paltry to me. Look at the animals, I said, they don't only have two legs, they have four. When we talk about an animal, be it horse or snail or weasel, do we also say it walked over here, it walked over there? We then realized that we have a special name for the way almost every type of animal moves. Something else dawned on the children at this point: Man can imitate every animal's gait. We proceeded to act this out as we said aloud (and later wrote down): "I trot like a colt; I strut like a peacock; I crawl like a snail. I scamper away like a little mouse. I slink around the corner like a fox. I waddle like a duck. I hop like a sparrow. I slither like a snake."

Man can imitate all animals, how they move, but no animal on earth can copy even for an instant how man strides upright across the earth, his arms free. We can only imitate what we already carry hidden within us and sometimes bring to light just for the fun of it. People and ducks can waddle; people and mice scamper away (how readily the children wanted to demonstrate these skills!). But it is not so good if a person is overly clever at wriggling through life; it is bad if someone is as flighty as a butterfly; and nobody likes a cunning fox who knows how to slink around every corner.

What do you do, what does every man do, with the mouth? He eats. Of course, so do animals. But he can speak, as well, and that's something animals cannot do. Another source of amazement: only man can speak. And animals? Well, that cannot be put in such general terms, for the lion roars, the cat meows, the wolf howls, the hen cackles, the cricket chirps, the frog croaks and the snake hisses. All of this, the roaring, the meowing, the cackling, man can imitate (the children were immediately ready to do so!). But only man can speak. The jungle cries of the animals confront the voices of a flock of attentive third graders reciting in chorus.

Until now (and we are far beyond the first grammar class) the children had always spoken of or meant themselves. Now it was time to acquaint them with the deeds of others. When one person stands opposite another and watches him, he can say to him, You are doing this and you are doing that. I know what you are doing. You are writing a long letter, you are painting a beautiful picture. Although the two of us belong together, we are often doing different things. In fact, quite frequently you are doing the opposite of what I am doing. I question and you answer. I work and you rest. I cry and you laugh. I speak and you are silent. I come and you go. To "Fingerhütchen" (we were then learning C.F. Meyer's poem of the same name) we said: You stand there before us with your humpback, a funny little hat you wear on your head. You do us no harm. We know well what you do. You cut the reeds along the brook; out of the reeds you weave baskets; you carry the baskets into town; on the way home you help the elves sing a song to its end.

Often, however, we talk to one person about a third person who is not even present. Be quiet, I may say, *he* is asleep, *he* has worked hard, now *he* is tired and is resting.

In this way we learned to become conscious of the first, second and third person singular and plural forms of the verb.

The verb also has other functions, however, It conceals and reveals the secrets of time, which is why it is also called *Zeitwort (timeword)* in German. If the teacher immerses himself in the time aspect of the verb (and Rudolf Steiner makes abundant suggestions), he will realize that the verb is presenting him with a special opportunity to make the child aware of himself in a threefold way.

When "handling" time, it is obvious that the present should come first. The child is, after all, a being of the present both in his deeds and in his attitude toward the environment. He savors the present. The bond he has formed to it through his feelings is extremely intense.

The child also lives intensively in the *future*, although through quite different forces than the feelings. Here it is quite clearly the will forces that are at work. Is it not true that the correct form of the future using the auxiliary verb "to be" is not at all common, and that this verb is replaced by another important verb, namely "to will?"

I *will* swim across the river (instead of: I *shall* swim across the river.

I will ride the wild horse.

I will climb to the top of the mountain.

I will! I will! I will! Always in the sense of I shall do it! But the will forces that point toward the future force their way forward, overwhelm the verb "to be" and put in its place the expression of pure will. Let us examine the difference between the present and the future.

1. I swim across the river (present).

The waters carry me, they wash against my body, I feel the coolness of the water; the delicate scent of the water reaches my nostrils, and the waves that looked so small from the dock are suddenly so big; my exhilaration is heightened by a tinge of fear. My body, my limbs are cool from the water, but the sun beats down on my head. Above me the blue sky, in front of me the green dock with reeds and brush. I swim and swim and breathe deeply.

2. I will swim across the river (future).

I am still standing on the dock. All the vivid pictures are erased. I simply let myself be guided by the will forces in me.

It made a great impression on the children when one after the other they were allowed to come to the front, take a firm step, look boldly ahead and say what they will do.

If the child experiences the "future" in this way, then he becomes strong as a willing being. He grasps the being of will in himself, whose physical, organic basis is the interaction of limbs and metabolism.

Now, what about the past? Recalling "yesterday" already presupposes certain powers of memory which the small child lacks as yet. Reviewing, judging and connecting "yesterday" with "today," however, requires powers of reflection. Once again we feel that quite a different soul force is active here than in the present and future, namely a thinking that looks back at the past—the forces of the head. The man of nerves and senses faces us.

I reflect upon events of bygone times.

"You already know a great deal," I said to the children, "about the secrets of the past. Biblical stories of creation! You may not know everything yet, but you know a great deal. Think about all that for a moment." The children thought. The responses did not come so quickly. A peculiar, pensive tension reigned. Some children, and it was almost comical to watch, had bowed their heads like ruminating old men reflecting on past deeds.

If the man of will approaches us through the verb, then the entire threefold man comes forward through the three tenses. Through them the child has become aware of himself in a threefold way. He has exercised threefold self-knowledge in an elementary, that is in an appropriate, way.

Instead of saying more about this segment of grammar I will quote the mnemonic about the three tenses exactly as the children copied it into their grammar books:

In the *present* I look around me,
With bright eyes and feeling soul.
I do what my heart demands.

Into the *future* I look bravely.
Good deeds will I do!
Yes, goodness and beauty will be my goals!
Strong be my will!

Into the *past* I look back.
With pensive soul,
Pondering mind.
From it I want to learn to stand in the present,
rightly and squarely,
So that I can do good
That lasts into the future.

After this came a somewhat more difficult segment. Rudolf Steiner repeatedly pointed out the importance of making the children aware of the difference between the imperfect and the perfect tense. What is this difference? Is it even that important? Continuing where we left off before, let us use a mundane example to make what follows perfectly clear. I can say both, "I ate lunch" (imperfect) and, "I have eaten lunch" (perfect). Both sentences express an event in the past. The relationship to the past, as well as to the present, however, is quite different each time. With the imperfect, something happened some place, some time that no longer has any special connection to the present. With the perfect, on the other hand, the event has just taken place a moment ago. The imperfect expresses the past as such, and it has no relationship to a beginning or to an end. Pictorially, it is like a river travelling far in the distance without visible beginning or end. The imperfect seeks no tie with the present and therefore makes no direct personal contact with us. Fairy tales *begin* with the imperfect: Once upon a time there lived a King!

The perfect is another story entirely. It stresses the ending point of an action; it tells us that something has happened, has come to an end, and that precisely for this reason something new can begin, right now, this instant. In a way, it challenges me to do something new. "I have eaten lunch"; that activity is thus over; we can move on to another activity. Where is the end of this so-called perfected past? Right where we are standing. It lays its hands on our shoulders and says, Whether perfect or not, done is done. The road is clear for new deeds (and to set past actions right!). It does not just say, I did wrong. It says, I have done wrong, but today I will try to make up for it. And how do German fairy tales *end*? "And if all have not died, they still live today." Thus, fairy tales begin with what appears to be the distant imperfect, move through the perfect and end with the immediate present in order to challenge us to right presence of mind.

The more the teacher studies these fine, but ever so meaningful distinctions during his preparatory work, the more he may grasp the importance of making the child aware of the different natures of these two forms of the past. Not only is the capacity for extremely subtle logic awakened in the child, but his consciousness is actually led to self-consciousness in a way commensurate with this age. Younger school children can quite easily be led to sense this difference. They already somehow feel the tendency that lies in the perfect tense when they can form sentences such as: I have written the letter, and now I am taking it to the post office. The children have had a swim in the Rhein and now they are getting dressed. The farmer has plowed the field, and now he can begin with the harrowing.

A new world opens with the adjective and yet another with the noun. The teacher, if he wishes to teach grammar in the proper way, should first discover for himself the inner relationships of the three kinds of words. If he spares no effort in so doing, then his reward is the wonderful experience of awakening to these three kinds of words in a threefold way, of learning how verb, adjective and noun enclose the power to call forth the will, thought and sentient feelings.

Try reading a poem or even a prose passage aloud to

yourself with special emphasis on the adjectives. Read them in a particularly "beautiful" way, surrendering your soul to them (you can do this with adjectives, but only with adjectives!), or even better, repeat them two or three times. With rhythmic repetition you will soon notice that they push themselves to the forefront.

The beginning of a piece of prose out of a reader will serve as a simple example and small exercise (I have written each adjective twice).

"On a hot, hot summer day, a small, small cloud rose out of the blue, blue sea and drifted like a glowing, playing child across the blue, blue sky over the wide, wide land scorched, oh how scorched by the long, long drought."

Whoever reads this single sentence out loud will immediately feel how adjectives are particularly powerful in conjuring up feeling. They are the true feeling-words. You could say they have a purely vocalic nature; they easily lead us (provided we are not unfeeling idiots) into the *Ah!*, *Oh!* or *Ow!* mood. That is what characterizes adjectives, the fact that they evoke a mood. We express our moods with feeling-packed qualifiers.

Because they carry the mood within themselves, adjectives are the true mood-makers in human speech. All adjectives are by nature interjections, that is, cries of the sensitive human being.

The nature of adjectives—they ought to be called feeling-words—becomes even clearer when you let the children read a prose passage in unison with special stress on the adjectives. The children immediately feel how fraught with feeling these words are, and they shout them out into the world with joy and enthusiasm. They feel deeply related to them. The adult is much more likely than the still healthy child to overdo a good thing by using the adjectives to wallow in emotion. Is man still capable of strong feelings such as reverence or the awfulness of an event? Take, for example, the phrase, It was *awfully* nice of you to come.

We also told one another stories: Once upon a time there was a sweet, good child, who wanted to go into the forest to pick a beautiful flower. It was for her good, good mother who was so, oh so ill. So she went into the dark, gloomy forest. All of a sudden, what did she see? A merry, merry squirrel! Oh, what a bushy, bushy tail it had!—(Later the grim, grim wolf came with blood-red tongue and sharp, pointy teeth. But the good, loyal hunter was also nearby, and the oh so feeling-laden story ended well and happily after all.)

I was not at all surprised that the adjective made the children clamor for colored pencils so they could present everything in color. They wanted to use color to express visibly the feelings that the adjectives had aroused in them. They wanted to draw the golden cornfield and the red, red poppy.

During the class the adjective increasingly revealed itself as the feeling-word through the behavior of the children themselves. The forces of sympathy and antipathy lie in it, the world of contrast, the numerous nuances of good and evil. The children themselves demanded to find this contrast in a constantly changing kaleidoscope of colors, in

beautiful and ugly
smart and dumb,
lazy and diligent
cowardly and brave
white and black.

In the process they experienced their own feelings in a living interplay of sympathy and antipathy. They became aware of the feeling man inside them.

The fact that feelings can intensify, that something can be beautiful, something else even more beautiful, but that of all the many beautiful things in the world something can be the most beautiful, that Snow White is the most beautiful in the whole land, was self-evident to the children. They experienced the intensification of the adjective as an intensification of feeling.

How completely different are the nouns. What are they, anyway? Names, mere names! I give names to the things that I perceive with the sense organs in my head. Here I stand as the neutral observer, and there are the things, which I register, file, name. My will is almost completely still, my feelings are silent. I am only a perceiving being. My head alone is "active," but in a passive way. The German word for noun, *Hauptwort* (literally "head-word"), is thus quite correct.

The noun does not look at the quality of things. Therefore it does not pass judgment like the adjective. It does, however, notice the quantity, the amount, like an official who registers a family during a census. As an official he may not concern himself with who among these family members is a man of honor and who a rogue, who a genius and who an idiot. He is just charged with counting them. Similarly, the noun also distinguishes between singular and plural. It makes neither a moral nor an aesthetic judgment. In some languages, in addition to number it also registers the external relationship of things to one another. In German this is expressed in the four cases nominative, accusative, dative and genitive.

Through the action-word we live in the middle of world events, through the feeling-word we are still instinctively bound to the environment, through the head-word, however, we isolate ourselves from this environment and confront it knowingly as a self-reliant being. Through the verb we live in the world of morality, through the adjective in the world of esthetics, but through the noun we stand in the realm of pure conception, that is, beyond good or evil, beautiful or ugly.

Compare and reflect on the following sets of words:

To do something ugly—to be ugly—ugliness,
To create something beautiful—to be beautiful—beauty.

The two examples show us three stages. They lead from the most concrete action to the most abstract allegory. They lead from the hands and feet through the heart up to the head.

I can still say: How *beautiful* is the *ugliness* painted by this painter! This means that with the nouns I stand beyond moral and esthetic judgment. I am in the world of pure thought and intellect. Nothing is left but the name. The last trace of life is expressed by the cases, which allow the noun to form a connection to the environment.

It came about quite naturally during the class that we first listed names, nothing but names. Adam gave all things their name.

But who gave Adam his name?

Every child has his own name. Write down all the people's names that you know. You may also write down the names of all the trees. And write the names of all the animals in your book, too.

Don't the angels have names, too? And the God of Moses?

Just names, nothing but names. The most abstract thing you can imagine.

But there are such strange stories like "Rumpelstiltskin," to name just one. The bad little spirit wanted to steal the queen's child, and it had the power to do so. But as the queen called the nasty spirit by his proper name, he lost all power over her and the child. Yes, he split himself in two from top to bottom, which goes to show how good it would be to know the proper name for all things (the key word being "proper"). These things would then reveal their true being—and we would stand in the world in the right way with our deeds and with our feelings.

★ ★ ★

I will close with the mnemonics that the children wrote in their exercise books at the end of this segment of grammar.

I have my limbs:
so that I can stand in the world, so that I can do something to help other people to create beauty, to create things that were not there before and that would not be there without me. I run, I swim, I paint, I knit, I write a letter, I sow and plant.

I have my heart:
With my heart I feel what is around me. My heart expresses what it feels, what it likes and what it dislikes. My heart says: Oh, how beautiful! Ah, how splendid! Ooh, how dark! Ugh, how dirty! Gee, how nice! Ow, how rough!

I have my head:
I perceive the things that are around me. Here am *I* and there are the things. The head does nothing to the things, it doesn't even say whether it likes them or dislikes them. It says only: There they are and that is what they are called. That is the tree, that the stone, that the ox and that the donkey, that is the devil and that the angel.

Teaching History

Everything the teacher does in the classroom can have only *one* purpose, that of educating the children entrusted to him. The subjects themselves allow the teacher to realize this purpose. These seem to be banal, uncontested truths. Even when we go one step farther and ask what the goal of education is, we still do not leave such truisms behind. Everyone will answer that, of course, the *entire* man should be educated. In his pedagogical writings Troxler says, The child gives himself to his teacher for better or for worse, but with complete faith that with the teacher's help he will become him*self* with increasing certainty and definition.

Those truly concerned only with education, and luckily they are still many, will realize that this statement by the educator Troxler is also a truism. This realization, however, makes new demands on the teacher, for he must now understand the living conditions under which this self can develop in a child according to its own predisposition. Depending on the extent to which the teacher is able to recognize and enhance these conditions for growth, and adjust his teaching accordingly, his teaching will have a healing or harmful effect. To a large degree—whether the teacher likes it or not—he holds in his "hand" the power to make the child's self healthy and strong or to weaken it. True pedagogy is nothing less than a doctrine of health. It deals not only with the child's physical body, but with his entire being, and it is only meaningful when it is put into practice, when knowledge is increasingly transformed into ability.

This self that everyone possesses has three sides expressed by the three basic powers of thinking, feeling and willing. Only when all three basic powers are unfolded in the proper way can we seriously speak of education. Perhaps this recognition has also become general knowledge. After all, the real difficulties arise only when we attempt to implement our knowledge in the classroom. Why? Because the routine of our daily lives hardly equips us to understand the threefold aspect of the human self. Yet, before we strive to educate someone we must have a glimmer of understanding for his true being.

We feel most confident in the realm of thinking. Therefore, it seems relatively easy to school the child's thinking forces. There are countless psychological studies and experiments on perception and thinking. Those on feeling are much scarcer. Here the uncertainty begins, for by their nature these forces elude experimentation and even escape mere speculative observation. Moreover, indulging in feelings and living knowingly in them are two entirely different things. It is a fact (not all that difficult to recognize) that feeling, as opposed to thinking, represents another element of consciousness. This is why it simply slips away from the awake intellect and the experiment it devises. In terms of degree of consciousness, feeling is just as far removed from rational awakeness as is the dream consciousness into which we slip each night. Every serious attempt to research the nature of feeling shows that it would be possible only if the researcher were willing to risk performing the change of consciousness experiment on himself.

But what do we know about the will forces? If we are to be completely honest and stop deluding ourselves, then we must admit that we know nothing about them, absolutely nothing. It is an illusion to mistake the external reactions of the will forces, which we can perceive and determine via experiment, for the will itself. These forces seem to be especially impervious to our typical, intellectual consciousness. We know as little about them as we "know" about the dreamless deep sleep. When we try to pin down the will forces, the knowledge may arise in us that doing so would require an even deeper state of consciousness, one even further removed from waking consciousness. Our knowledge would have to be transformed and strengthened in a way barely dreamed of.

The first result of the educator's preoccupation with these problems is an important recognition: his own self, the way it lives in his thinking, feeling and willing, achieves three qualitatively different degrees of consciousness. Out of these the requirement for a threefold transformation of our cognitive capacity could arise.

It is precisely because today's psychology must fail at this point that pedagogy is so difficult to put into practice. For psychology determines pedagogy, which in turn determines methodology and didactics. Therefore, today's classroom instruction, despite the teachers' better judgment, must reluctantly be limited to educating the intellectual forces, even if the teacher tries to address the feeling forces at the same time. Education of the will, however, is left primarily to gymnastics and sports. Such is the general educational situation today. This is also why, in spite of occasional denials, the subject matter simply serves to enrich intellectual knowledge. The goal is to store the greatest possible amount of knowledge in the child, so that later, during his daily routine, he can withdraw it as needed. This is why the subject matter has lost its rightful meaning. It has lost its power.

Anthroposophy as psychology, however, can restore the true meaning of the subject matter. It gives the teacher the chance to develop a true inner pedagogy, not as mere system of education, but as actual teaching practice.

With this kind of pedagogy the subject matter no longer means enrichment of knowledge, but once again serves its original purpose as tool for education. It becomes clear to the teacher that the subjects are there to strengthen and stimulate the three basic powers in each child. It is then the teacher's task to realize the ideal meaning of the subject matter. How successful he is depends on his own development potential.

This viewpoint justifies the question, What is the educational importance of history? I will try (also within my own development potential) to answer that question. It will be a one-sided answer, in other words, I will try to make only *one* side of the problem somewhat clearer.

Perhaps some of you will ask whether it is even possible for history, as educational tool, to live up to this tough standard. Can history be taught in school in order to promote life?

Almost 150 years ago Friedrich Nietzsche published "The Use and Abuse of History for Life." The educator today can reap only the greatest benefit from this little book because it forces him to cope with these problems. We know that the author has no shortage of negative things to say about history's effect on mankind. Modern man (at least the modern European), miseducated by the subject of history (in its excess) and with a weakened life-force, "drags around with him a huge quantity of indigestible stones of knowledge, which then . . . can sometimes be heard rumbling about inside him."[15] As in the fairy tale, "the expulsion of the instincts by history has transformed men almost into mere *abstractis* and shadows."[16] Yes, says Nietzsche, history as taught in our schools has almost reduced us to walking encyclopedias, flesh-and-blood compendia. We carry an enormous amount of knowledge around with us, but it lacks the power to give our life the form it deserves. This knowledge in itself, this heap of mere stones, has buried the true human powers. Small wonder that the health of the individual, like the health of the entire nation, was destroyed by textbook history. Nietzsche then asks himself a question that seems of tremendous importance to him: "How [can] the health of a people undermined by the study of history . . . be restored again?"[17] And his answer, as we have seen, is: "A hygiene of life belongs close beside science . . ."[18] But the remedies that this hygiene administers are the unhistorical and the suprahistorical.

Thus the situation appeared in Nietzsche's time, and thus the life-line that he threw his contemporaries. Where do we stand today? Has life-destroying textbook history been attacked and rendered harmless? What does a hygiene of life mean? Surely only a true pedagogy. Where is it? Where are the young people strengthened and able to deal with life by means of the unhistorical and the suprahistorical? Where are the teachers who know how to implement such a hygiene of life?

A doctor uses symptoms to determine whether his patient is healthy or ill. He differentiates between symptoms of recovery and deterioration.

In the United States, lesson plans state that the "acquisition of good encyclopedia and notebook habits" is one of the "most important goals of teaching." Symptom of deterioration! True, America is far from here (Switzerland), and an ocean separates us. In an educational treatise, however (to name another symptom), written by a German professor of Psychology and Pedagogy and consultant to a Ministry of Education, we find claims such as these: "The student who does not learn how to use the modern encyclopedia will be unable to meet life's demands—Teaching the encyclopedia is a valuable, even indispensable part of the ultimate preparation for real life."

What is being advocated here is teaching children the

encyclopedia. Symptom of deterioration! The devil that Nietzsche conjured up to throw a good scare into his contemporaries is evoked here as an ideal figure. But the devil is a flesh-and-blood encyclopedia! He is visible in the classroom, pacing back and forth in front of the desks, as the large Britannica or Americana or Webster's called teacher, and sitting behind the desks in front of him, the smaller Britannica or Americana called pupil.

People dedicated to true education are appalled at these educational goals. They are well aware that the more a child adopts good encyclopedia habits, the more he is cut off from his life-force. How can figures of alleged authority lack such basic pedagogical insights? The obvious answer is that these people are not yet aware of a hygiene of life; they are not educators and have no idea how the three basic powers work in man; they themselves are walking encyclopedia and would gladly see nothing but people like themselves. The tragedy, however, is that such flesh-and-blood encyclopedia are considered authorities and are invited to lecture at influential conferences where their opinions are accepted.

Here a temptation can become quite great. Why should children be burdened with history at all, you may ask yourself. Why can't a child grow up uninhibited by the burden of the past? That way he cannot be estranged from life and will at any time be able to follow his natural inclination as an unhistorical being. Two extremes confront one another: On the one hand, the mummified encyclopedia, on the other, the unhistorical animal, i.e. the human being. Neither one can be the ideal goal of education, as lovable as a completely unhistorical human being might be. Josephine Baker was perhaps such a kind, completely unhistorical being, unspoiled by an excess of historical knowledge. Strangely enough, however, she still wrote her memoirs, or rather made it possible for a journalist to do so. Of course, these memoirs are light as gossamer, not weighing much more than the costumes Josephine donned each time she stepped on the stage. But she also made this amusing remark, among others: "What I would like to own now is a big encyclopedia in seven volumes! I will never even open it, I have no time for that. But I would weigh each volume in my hands and laugh myself sick over it. I need all my time for living."

A human encyclopedia cannot be more categorically disavowed than with those words by Baker. But we see the contrasts: on the one hand, the unhistorical man; he must live, therefore he has no time at all to deal with history in any shape or form. On the other hand, the man who has lost the ability to think other than historically; he slaves away in the service of history and thereby loses his life.

Nietzsche, however, makes demands on the unhistorical-suprahistorical man, one whose life has not been devoured by the dragon of history, but who has used the past as a nourishing food to become strong and able to cope with life. Hence the demand for a hygiene of life, which belongs close beside science. Has Nietzsche the diagnostician progressed to therapist? Has he shown educators a *path*, a *method*? For everything, after all, depends on education! It can prevent more people from walking around in the near future as flesh-and-blood compendia under the false banner of "human being." Once reduced to a compendium it is not so easy for an already existing, fully-grown being to become human again. To do so he would have to give up his compendium existence, and who likes to give up his existence?

What we find in Nietzsche is not a path, not an educational method, but valuable suggestions. These can be trailblazers for the teacher, indicating the general direction in which to proceed. Later the wanderer might become confused again and lose his way just as Nietzsche himself did.

An example of such trailblazing, valuable words, as the readers will remember is:

> If you are to venture to interpret the past you can do so only out of the fullest exertion of the vigor of the present: only when you put forth your noblest qualities in all their strength will you divine what is worth knowing and preserving in the past. Like to like! Otherwise you will draw the past down to you.[19]

It must, of course, always be remembered that when Nietzsche speaks of "history," he does not mean it only in the narrow sense of subject or scientific field. For him history is the expression and symbol of a particular way of thinking and conducting research, or, when applied to pedagogy, the expression of a particular teaching method. He must reject it because it stems from a very one-sided and otherwise suspect human faculty, the pure intellect. Therefore, there is a warning underlying Nietsche's words: Do not venture to approach history in your usual state of mind, with your routine consciousness. That way you may grasp the routine of daily life, but not the thoughts, deeds and passions of a bygone humanity.

The validity and trailblazing nature of such suggestions can be confirmed by Anthroposophy. Anthroposophy as path of spiritual knowledge enables us (not without great struggle) to discard gradually that part of us that is merely an abstract of existence or life in name only, thereby making room for a more real, spiritual existence. It shows *how* these most noble forces of which Nietzsche speaks can blossom in the educator. It leads us to an understanding of the past and enables us to read its documents. Gradually we perceive the true face of world history. It is important to mention here that when thus tracing the path of history, we are not eventually pulled down to the caveman (as a death-oriented theory of history would have it), and then even farther down in a peculiar leap to the animal. Instead, we ascend to ancient civilizations, the ancient Indians, Persians, Egyptians, and Greeks, and to their great leaders, the holy Rischis, Zarathustra, Hermes, etc. After first recognizing how any intellectual arrogance, in addition to being criminally naive and limited, also stifles our understanding, we are amazed, moved and awed by the ancient documents.

It is as though there were people once who, without great effort or mighty striving, participated in the highest spirituality and divinity. Compared to these people we must see ourselves as desperately poor today—poor in spirit. We recognize that we people of today must arduously and step by step come to awarenesses from the inside that came to an earlier people from the outside like a shining revelation and like something quite natural.

The farther back we follow the history of man, the higher, we feel, is his spiritual culture. But the higher it goes, the less we can understand it with our ordinary powers of reasoning. Less and less can we, as mere modern-day men, arrive at the right standpoint with regard to such a completely different kind of knowledge. At every moment we are literally at our wits' end. We do not even have to go back to the very beginning of human history to discover the limitations of our rational knowledge. Out of the not so distant past, which we call the Middle Ages, something blows towards us that we cannot rationally understand. The influences still present in the Middle Ages, which we may thus call the Real, slip through the net of the intellect. What gets caught in the net is no longer the Real. Should anyone insist on using it to write history, it will inevitably be a counterfeit history. But then, history counterfeiting is a thriving business today.

If we trace human history as far back as we possibly can,

then we see how in the end it changes into mythology. Today's intellect is already so far removed from mythology that, as long as with unique narrowness it considers only itself valid, it must label mythology as unreal and therefore as untrue.

A nation's myths, however, can express the force of consciousness and the knowledge potential only of that nation. It clearly follows that the consciousness of mankind has changed over the years not just in terms of scope, but in terms of quality. Whoever still believes that a farmer in ancient Persia felt and thought similarly (just somewhat more "primitively") to today's farmer, for him world history is a closed book, he turns world history into counterfeit history; he has pulled the past down to himself, and has heedlessly brought it down to a level that he himself is not prepared to leave.

We cannot really progress, however, by regarding our present consciousness as the non plus ultra and by chipping away at a past epoch of human development until, at the expense of reality, we have brought it down to our own level of consciousness. The only way to progress (which brings Nietzsche to mind) is by bringing to the forefront of our awareness a force that, though buried, is available to us all. We will thereby be able to understand the change in consciousness that history reveals to us. This is the only way to overcome history and to turn the past into the present in the true sense. The history of mankind is the history of a change in consciousness. To understand that history we must ourselves undergo a change of consciousness, or at least have some idea of what that would mean.

It is important that the teacher gradually become aware that, in addition to this change in consciousness of all mankind, another change is taking place to which he is the constant eyewitness. This one occurs in the life of the individual, in every single child that matures before the teacher's eyes.

I can only call upon all of you to observe objectively. Anyone still capable of this must notice how, for example, the small child is not dumber than we are, but simply experiences the environment with another consciousness (and much more intensely than the adult). He must see how the intellectual cognitive capacity develops slowly as the result of the most diverse metamorphoses. Why is it that we so often disregard these changes in the child? Because we attribute our own completed state of consciousness to the child. We then treat what has arbitrarily been *made* seemingly equal to ourselves as equal or similar in principle, though supposedly more primitive. In addition, we allow ourselves to be misled by what the child, as an imitative being, picks up from the adult on a superficial level.

The same weakness and rigidity of intellectual thinking prevents us from understanding first the development of mankind as a whole and then the development of an individual child. The result is a history and pedagogy that distorts reality. As the teacher becomes attuned to subtleties he missed before and adjusts his teaching accordingly, Anthroposophy as pedagogy and psychology enables him to experience imaginatively and to understand intellectually the transformations in a child. The more successful the teacher is in adopting the proper pedagogical attitude toward a child, the more that child will reveal his true being to him. The same child can behave completely differently toward two adults, but one of those times he will not be himself at all. The teacher may then also begin (and this is only mentioned in passing) to watch himself and to trace his own development back to his earliest childhood. Minor events that are quite trivial for others then become so alive again that he may say, I do not remember them in the usual sense; in reliving these events I am experiencing them more or less the same way I did as a child. They can be very important experiences pedagogically speaking, even when they concern, as we said, "trivialities." Take the following concrete examples from real life: At the age of five, a particular individual climbed to the top of a crooked (thus easily climbable) pear tree and let the wind rock him; another time he sat at the edge of a brook so the water could flow over his bare feet; or he stood in the dark village smithy watching for the first time the fire blazing in the forge.

What is important here is not so much the picture someone remembers of being fanned by a breeze, bathed by water or heated by flames, but that through these remembrances (they are only examples) he reexperiences the elements with the same intensity and quality that he did as a child. He then realizes how far this ordinary adult consciousness has separated him from his consciousness as a child. He experiences in a very real way the change in consciousness that has occurred within himself.

Out of such insights the knowledge arises in the teacher that he can best prepare his children for history with the myths, the stories of the gods. They are not yet history, but they give birth to history. To the cold intellect, of course, they are an inaccessible garden, and walls erected by the intellect itself hide that garden from view. But there are many people who are still able, or have newly learned, to peek over the walls, and they find the garden very beautiful. Whoever should succeed in entering, however, would find, clad in beauty and imagery, truth and reality in the making.

The unspoiled child lives quite naturally in the world of mythology and of the fairy tale. His attitude toward the stories about gods is not esthetic, but quite concrete. He experiences their truth by virtue of a still innate consciousness related to the consciousness that speaks out of myths.

After the age of ten, however, myth and saga can gradually turn into history even for a child.

Here one question must be answered that is not without bearing on education. Should history be introduced more narrowly, as national history, or more broadly, as world history? In most countries the teacher is probably instructed to begin with national history. This reflects a very specific view on the meaning and purpose of education: to turn the developing human being into a good citizen. According to this theory man exists for the sake of the state, not the other way around. It is still not all that long ago that the great educator Pestalozzi was openly eulogized all over civilized Europe. Thus, for an educator today to consider seriously words spoken and written by Pestalozzi cannot be out of place. At this juncture there are two, to some probably very familiar statements by Pestalozzi I would like to quote, because they transcend casual issues and present the quintessence of his educational insights and activity.

> Man is more man than citizen, and the education of man must find its purpose in itself.

> If the people are to find pleasure in themselves and become self-conscious as a nation as well, elementary schools must not promote the individual national character, or still less a specific class and profession, but the general human character. (Lenzburg speech)

From such insights it follows that the study of history should be a history of mankind, a journey through all epochs of civilization until the "present"; it should be a world history in which the history of one's own people is legitimately included. What the children gain in world awareness and breadth of world knowledge, through which they learn to face the world's phenomena objectively, more than makes up for any time that is "lost" (as they are forever saying) for narrower national history. Could anyone not find such objectivity a worthy goal of education?

For those worried about patriotism, an extra word: The history of a particular people can be understood only when it is experienced as imbedded and included in the historical development of mankind as a whole. It will never be understood if it is studied by and for itself, as though no other peoples had once pursued or would ever pursue their own mission and experience the flowering of their civilization. It will never be understood as long as the history of these peoples is treated as worthless for education except, at best, as a supplement to the history of one's own country, as mere decorative addition to one's own momentary dwelling. The path to understanding the history of any people winds its way through the history of mankind as a whole. Why? Because the concept of "mankind" is no more an empty abstraction than the concept of "nation" or "national spirit." All are very concrete "ideas."

Whoever is not allowed to walk this legitimate path of history with the children, whoever is obliged to begin with the history of his own people, should first allow his children to spend some time living and breathing in the mythological world of this people. The history and purpose of the Germanic people, for example, will remain a locked door without the key of Germanic mythology. It makes just as little sense, to use another example, of trying to teach children Greek history without having prepared them for it through Greek heroic sagas and stories about the gods. True, it is essential that the teacher not have a merely esthetic or primarily emotional attitude toward such myths, but that he can penetrate them consciously. Anthroposophy is a path to this goal.

He who has been given the gift of freedom in his teaching, on the other hand, would most certainly do well to begin with world history. In other words, begin with the oldest civilization, the ancient Indians, in order from there to move via the Persians and Babylonians to the ancient Egyptians. Then it is no longer far to the Greeks.

What comes to light first for the teacher who spares no expense of time and energy in devoting himself intensely to the history of these ancient people? He sees that every new civilization was inaugurated by one exceptional person who stood out from the rest. Through his work new social conditions are created. What later generations all experience, *he* first experiences in his unrivaled power and greatness. These are the leaders of men in pre-Christian times. Are they men or gods? The epic calls Gilgamesh two-thirds god, one-third man! In all cases they are the beloved of the gods: Krishna, Zarathustra, Gilgamesh, Hermes.

It is imperative that the teacher overcome his fear of ancient history. Though understandable, this fear is truly no longer permitted. This is clear to anyone who has delved deeply (if only step by step) into ancient history, and now discovers the pedagogical aids it offers the teacher. But what causes this fear? The fact that through ancient history man is lead to civilizations that are in no way built on the human intellect as it is today, valid only for today. The teacher enters territory increasingly foreign to his rational consciousness. Once he overcomes this fear, however, he will discover forces growing within him with which he can knowingly penetrate the essence of these long gone civilizations. He can, for example, become so at one with the Baghavad-Gita that with his innermost being he feels somehow part of the events being expressed there. He no longer thinks "historically," as someone who is basically a non-participant, but feels in this seeming past the forces of an immediate present and of a distant future.

This is also the best preparation for teaching history. Indeed, it is the only opportunity to incorporate educational forces into the teaching of history. I, the teacher, am then also able to select what is typical, symptomatic or character-istic for a people or an entire cultural period and to structure it for the children in the proper way. I cannot, after all, recite them the entire Mahabharata, but I can tell them the legends of Krishna. The children absorb these stories and images in their soul and live very intensely in the Welt-anschauung of the ancient Indians, not with their intellects but with their feelings and sentiments. The experience of how the ancient Indians saw their relationship to the world and to the gods can be further enhanced by, for example, telling them of the life of Gautama Buddha. At first glance, this certainly seems to take us into a much later period of In-dian history. But if we observe the inner and outer attitude of the ancient Indians toward the entire earthly environ-ment, and how this attitude is perfectly expressed in Buddha, then we see that this later period is the last wonderful blossom of the whole Indian civilization.

What does a child experience, at first wholly with his feelings, when the teacher lets such stories, in which spiri-tual and earthly events, unseparated by any walls, still over-lap, speak to the child's soul? The child realizes that such people are not yet fully on the earth, that they live much more intensely in the heavenly or demonic worlds. They would therefore like best of all to escape this earth and enter the divine world. Their physical body and the earth on which they walk means nothing to them, but their soul and the kingdom of the Daevas means everything. It is as if they were constantly looking back into a lost paradise.

Those children, however, who are nearing perhaps the age of ten see (if not yet consciously) part of their own being in the feelings and behavior of the ancient Indians.

If we then take another step along the path of human his-tory, we encounter the ancient Persians. They lead us into a completely new world. I would like to shed light on their

totally different attitude toward the world, based on a quite
different consciousness, by means of a few concrete and perhaps lesser known examples. They appear here as the children in my class copied them into their history notebooks.
The only difference between what they wrote and the text
lying in front of me [Alfred Bertholet's *Die Zoroastrische
Religion*, published by K.F. Gelder, Tübingen, 1926] is the
length, theirs being somewhat shorter.

How does Zarathustra, the hero of the Persian people,
experience the divine world? How does it speak to him and
through him to all Persians? Thus speaks Zarathustra to
Ahura Mazdao, the creator of worlds:

Who is the first generator and upholder of righteous-
ness? Who determines the path of the sun and the stars?
Who is it through whom the moon waxes and wanes? . . .
Who is it that upholds the heaven and the earth from falling
down? Who [sustains] the waters and the plants? . . . What
great artificer made sleep and waking?[20] It is I, answers
Ahura Mazdao. My gown is made of the sun's rays. The
angels are my helpers.

Always working against me is Ahriman, the arch-con-
taminator, whose evil purposes I try to make good again
through the holy cosmic rhythm. He does not want the plants
to grow, the rivers to flow and the rain to fall from the
heavens. He wants to disrupt the ordered path of the heavenly bodies. He would like the stars to be extinguished, the
sun to be obscured, darkness to reign, and in the darkness
for men to do evil and malicious things. His gown is the
darkness and his wicked helpers are the Daevas.

What do the children who absorb such words experience? God and the divine spirits did not create this earth for
man to turn away from and hold in low esteem, nor for it to
be destroyed again by God's adversary, by Ahriman. That
Ahriman wants to destroy the work of the cosmic artisan

reveals the value and significance of the earthly world. We must not allow the cosmos to become a chaos. Out of these words speaks a great fighting spirit. In an unspoken call to battle, man is charged here with defending light against darkness, good against evil. A fighting spirit is expressed here that is absent in the Indian writings.

The Supreme Being, however, revealed himself to one man, Zarathustra, who saw Him and saw through the arch-deceiver. That is why Ahriman wanted to corrupt him. The story of Zarathustra's temptation is as follows:

From the northern regions came Ahriman, the Arch-Daeva. Thus spoke the villain Ahriman to his helper, the wicked Druj: "Druj, prepare yourself to corrupt Zarathustra." Druj, the evil, deceitful one, coiled herself around Zarathustra to corrupt him. But Zarathustra began to pray and Druj could no longer harm him. Her power shattered, she ran away. To Ahriman she ran and said: "Destroyer Ahriman, I cannot corrupt Zarathustra. Too magnificent is the righteous Zarathustra."

Zarathustra recognized in his spirit: "The false, evil Daevas are consulting about my death." He rose and continued on his way, unbroken by the evil spirit. Stones he carried in his hand, as big as a house. He received them from the world creator, Ahura Mazdao.

Then Ahriman himself stepped before Zarathustra and spoke to him thus: "Where on this earth, this wide, round earth with its distant boundaries, are you carrying those large stones?" Zarathustra answered him: "Evil Ahriman, until the future Saviour is born I will strike and destroy the evil works created by the Daevas." The evil creator Ahriman answered Zarathustra: "Do not destroy my creation, rather take my advice and renounce the religion of the Mazdao worshippers. Great power will I give you." Spitama Zarathustra replied: "I will not renounce the good religion of the

Mazdao worshippers as long as body, life and consciousness remain one."

Then Ahriman, the evil one, ran from that place. He said: "All the angels could not force me to leave against my will, but Zarathustra alone makes me leave against my will. He smites me with his prayers. His prayers are powerful and effective, like stones big as houses. He burns me with his prayers. He better than all others makes me flee this earth, he, Spitama Zarathustra, who alone chases me away."

After Zarathustra has overcome the temptation, he can teach mankind what God has revealed to him. It is a new task for a new people, a new attitude toward God and the world. Through him something new comes to pass. People begin to consider the earth the field for their work. The earth itself assigns them tasks. The holy Rischis still said that one must turn away from the emptiness of the external world and direct one's gaze inward. The ideals of the ancient Indians were the anachoret, the yogi and the philosopher. Zarathustra, however, sees the earth as God's creation and recognizes man's responsibility to continue God's work. He calls upon people to act with vigor, to settle down and create a new civilization. He gives them the plough as a gift of the gods. He, himself, is the first farmer and the husbandman. Agriculture is a ritual action. Thus he speaks to the people (but through him speaks Ahura Mazdao):

"The third place wherein the Earth feeleth the greatest joy . . . is the place whereon one of the followers of the law of ASHA soweth the most of corn, of grass, and the most of fruit . . . Where he watereth that ground which is dry, or draineth the too wet soil. Unhappy is the land that has long lain unsown of the seed from the sower and wants a good husbandman . . . He who would till the earth . . . with the left arm and with the right, unto him will she bring forth plenty of fruit."[21]

But the Daevas do not like it when man cultivates the soil. When there is grain, they sweat with fear; when the harvest comes in, they tear out their hair; when there is white flour, they howl with rage, and when there is dough for baking good bread, the daevas fairly burst in two.

"No one who eateth not hath strength to do the works of ASHA, strength to do the works of husbandry . . . With eating every material creature liveth; with not eating it dieth away."[22]

Zarathustra's task was to make his people competent to work the soil so that they could continue the work of creation. Zarathustra recognizes that without human participation Ahriman causes nature to go wild. If we ally ourselves with Ahura Mazdao, however, we can ennoble nature, both plants and animals. Out of the wild, rending wolf comes the loyal, watchful dog, but only if man first develops these good soul qualities in himself. The ennobled animals then become, and not only outwardly, man's helpers. Take the rooster:

What does the rooster call out every morning in the early light of dawn light? "Arise men, arise! Promise the best law and forswear the Daevas. That long-fingered Bush-yasta is coming over you." Sleepiness. As the dawn breaks she lulls the entire earthly world to sleep again with the words, "Sleep long, oh man, your time for sleep is not yet up."

"Do not sleep away the three best things: the well-thought Thought, the Word well-spoken, and the Deed well-done.[23] Sleep away the three worst things: the poorly thought Thought, the Word poorly spoken and the Deed poorly done."

It is obvious that the ancient Persians were raised to give thanks to fire as the earthly foundation of all human culture:

"Hold the fire as holy. It warms you, it bakes your bread, it helps you forge your plowshares. Feed the fire with dry firewood seasoned in heavenly light."

Through intense study of the Avesta and the Gathas the teacher gains the strength to create pictures that vividly present Zarathustra to the children's souls as king, military commander, farmer and husbandman.

These episodes out of ancient Persian literature are mentioned only as examples, and not to express any special love for *this* period in history.

Every cultural epoch introduces a new element into the development of the human race, and is therefore something unique. Hence, the study of world history allows the child to draw a special strength out of each one of these epochs, which no other can give him in such intensity and purity. The children receive a different strength from Indian history than from Persian, or from Egyptian history than from Greek. Just as each civilized race had its mission with respect to all of humanity, so does every race have its educational mission through its "history" for the developing human beings of the present. Here the meaning of history as educational tool becomes obvious.

Perhaps it is still necessary to address certain objections that could be made. You might ask yourself whether ancient history isn't too hard for children to understand. After all, it is hard enough for us adults to get a real grip on it. The answer is that it is only hard for us adults because to get close to the ancient civilizations, we must give up our dictionary existence. Children, on the other hand, do not first have to strip themselves of this existence; they are immediately open to what history brings them. That is why—and experience bears this out—history comes naturally to them. They are simply rediscovering themselves in it, if always in a new way. This explains their great interest precisely in ancient history.

It is not necessary, or even advisable, that the children grasp everything rationally (and this pertains especially to the first history block). "It is preferable for the child's will and feelings to be gripped, that is, he must be able to achieve a personal relationship to the historical figures, as well as to the depiction of life-styles in individual epochs of world history." (Rudolf Steiner.)

The history teacher should also be able to penetrate a mystery fruitful for teaching, which can perhaps be captured in these words: Great truths, which a child has absorbed with feelings of awe, joy or love, without "understanding" them, sink into the sleeping will precisely because they are not first intercepted by the intellect. There they lie, a living seed. Decades later they rise to the surface transformed into a living force for knowledge. Seen from this perspective, the history of the most ancient civilizations offers the child particularly great possibilities of development.

What is intercepted by the awake intellect will not sink into the depths of the child's soul, and can therefore no longer grow and transform itself. Instead, it turns into one of those indigestible knowledge-stones that are such a burden on modern man. This is the "historical thinking," which can spread only at the expense of life. From this perspective, we can really "identify" with Nietzsche when he says: "A man who wanted to feel historically through and through would be like one forcibly deprived of sleep . . ."[24]

The mystery of the sleep consciousness and that of the human will belong together. That Nietzsche was close to penetrating this mystery is borne out by these words: "[History can] deprive youth of its fairest privilege, of its power to implant in itself the belief in a great idea and then let it grow to an even greater one."[25]

Let us also try to refute yet another objection. Someone might ask, Couldn't a child become so attracted to one of the ancient cultural epochs that he can no longer free himself from it and gets stuck there? My response is that this is asked from a completely adult standpoint. The danger of getting stuck does indeed exist for today's adult, who has been deformed by history and whose life-force has been weakened. Perhaps he can no longer consciously cope with a present containing so little joy and has lost the strength to create anything for the future. Then he discovers a piece of the past that appeals to him. He takes it as *it* is and as *he* is and transports it unchanged into the present. Then, however, he is no longer free, but is subjugated by a piece of the past. He may then flirt with the "east," becoming a pseudo-Indian or neo-Buddhist. He may revive the teaching of Zarathustra and forget his most obvious life-tasks in the process. Put crudely, his life is then one big lie, for *this* is a truth:

> People are constantly saying that history should teach us something. It cannot, however, teach us anything by parading the past before us, but rather by enabling us to find something new in the hidden layers under human existence. (Rudolf Steiner)

That is what the child, without being aware of it himself, wants from history. The child wants to use the past like a powerful nutrient for his feeling, thinking and willing forces. For him, the epochs of history are stages of his own consciousness. He converts the past into the power to create something new once he becomes self-reliant.

The history teacher is faced with a great task and a great responsibility. Can he fulfill his task? What abilities must he develop? He must overcome his fear of ancient history. He must also overcome the historically noncommittal attitude toward history. History must be "binding" for him, yet may not bind him, or he will not be free from it. He may adopt no favorite cultural epoch or nation. He should experience the history of mankind as a history of a change in consciousness, not just as theoretical knowledge. This he can do only if he has reached the point where he recognizes at least in thought that his own consciousness might change. Moreover, he must be able to make the right choices and in due course to form the right images for the children. Demand upon demand! Perhaps the history teacher is being *over*taxed? Well, it is simply a fact that education—and I do not mean mere instruction—challenges the educator. The educator should at least not tire of striving to fullfil the tasks that life presents him. As paradoxical as it may sound, the strength to do so can be awakened in him by history itself.

The Main Lesson Block

The main lesson (cf. Translator's Preface) in Rudolf Steiner schools is divided into blocks. For a fairly long period of time (three to seven weeks) the same subject is taught every morning between 8:30 and 10:00. (The period between 8:00 and 8:30 being devoted to speech and recitation.) This schedule was suggested by Dr. Steiner and has been tested and practiced in all Rudolf Steiner Schools since their inception.

The division into blocks is first a blessing for the teacher. It enables him to concentrate on one main subject for several weeks and to feel completely at home with the material. He is thus able to present the subject matter to the child in a livelier and freer way than otherwise possible.

From the child's point of view the block method proves to be particularly important. Like the teacher, though out of a completely different state of consciousness, he can submerge himself in the world of a specific subject without constantly being wrenched out of that world by another main subject. The result of the fifty-minute class period, in a worst case scenario, is that each class nullifies the effect of the preceding one. But doesn't "block" instruction present a different kind of disadvantage? After all, once a block is over, it takes quite a while for that particular block and subject to be taught again, and it must then be linked somehow to what went before. During the long interim, haven't the children "slept away" and forgotten much of what they had learned before? This question can be answered through even brief experience. It is a great boon for a child to be allowed to "forget" something for a while. This boon is not just external, for—and it was Rudolf Steiner who suggested looking for these interrelations—the soul and spirit forces unfolded in the child during a main lesson block continue to work in him without human intervention, without the child's knowledge, and unnoticeable even to the teacher. It is precisely because of the lengthy rest period for each subject that what has been stimulated in the child by a main lesson block can transform itself, can ripen. This silent, undetected ripening during the rest period can reemerge as a deepened understanding when the same subject returns again and again in a certain rhythm. The rest periods built into the course of instruction have a similar importance for and impact on the instruction itself as has the sleep of man on the waking consciousness. The child is, as it were, grateful to you for not continuously holding him at attention in every subject. The block system gives him one less reason for anxiety.

The Life and Soul Metamorphoses of Man
and their Impact on Education

It is remarkable that interest in biographies has been growing by leaps and bounds in recent years. Admittedly, the first targets of this interest are the memoirs of figures prominent during the last decades, especially during World War II. It may, therefore, mean that much of this interest is based on common curiosity and thirst for the sensational.

We can see time and again, however, both in ourselves and in our contemporaries, that even the lives of those not directly involved in the events of the last decades hold a deep fascination for us. Often we are intrigued by the life stories of people who lived at the turn of the 18th and 19th centuries, and sensationalism is no longer at the root of this kind of interest. What drives us to the biographies of these people clearly has a completely different source. It stems from a yearning to glimpse something of the spiritual core of a human being as it is outwardly manifested, in ever new transformations, in the course of a particular life. As we are tracing, reliving and inwardly recreating one individual's life, we wish (some are more conscious of this than others) to approach the spiritual laws of development as expressed in this one individuality. There is, however, another factor. We suspect there may be spiritual laws that are presented slightly differently in each individual, but are nevertheless valid for all of humanity—meaning also for us, the readers of such biographies. We feel that if we learn to understand an unfamiliar biography (i.e. recognize the secret laws of transformation and development as revealed in one biography), then we have come one step closer to understanding our *own* biography. Knowledge of others should lead to self-knowledge. The drive for self-knowledge is the deepest, if often hidden, reason why biographies appeal to us so much, why we want to reexperience lives lived long ago.

These spiritual laws of transformation and development for which we are searching, however, do not lie on the surface of a biography—be it written, still unwritten, or even our own—and are not easily understood. What a human life reveals to us is at first a conglomeration of facts, more confusing than anything else, which we must accept as such, without being able to interpret them right away. I may, for example, experience through a biography how in one individual, in one particular year of his life, a soul force blossoms which did not seem to be there before, and which now gives his life a completely different, new direction; or an inadequacy may materialize at a certain point in this person's life, a weakness of the soul, which prevents him from structuring his life the way his entire being demands. We might then feel that where there should be a living force there is instead a void, a dead nothingness. Rather than looking at a man's soul and spirit, however, I can also look at his physical makeup, and perhaps I am astounded at such a man's physical health, which lets him enjoy a trouble-free old age. But a biography may also show that, in a certain phase of its development, a particular organ becomes diseased, seemingly without cause. I am then forced to watch how someone with an apparently strong constitution becomes a diabetic, or asthmatic, or is prematurely afflicted by sclerosis.

The biography yields this kind of surface information. But if I ask questions such as, Where do abilities of soul and spirit originate? What does the seed look like that becomes visible when transformed into a flower? Why do we see withering and atrophy instead of the awaited soul force? Where do the tendencies lie that later appear as physical health or organic disease?—then the biography, both written and unwritten, has no answers. The secret laws that work at the center of every man's life must remain hidden to the first superficial observation. If I try to trace these life and soul metamorphoses, for this is what we are dealing with, I soon notice that my usual, purely conceptual thinking lacks the necessary strength. I realize very quickly that in order to follow the seed's hidden transformations into flower and fruit, I must transform my thinking itself; I must make it more alive and active. But is there a path leading to this kind of living thinking?

Searching for these hidden laws of transformation a man could then be fortunate enough to read Goethe's *Metamorphosis of the Plant.* Now he sees the essential being of the plant through Goethe's eyes. He sees how all the vastly different plant parts manifest one and the same supraphysical basic force. Thus, he recognizes the secret relationship between seed, stem, leaf and flower. Seen through Goethe's eyes, all of these are the physical expression of a higher supraphysical oneness, which chooses to come into external existence in ever new transformations. The fortunate reader then sees implemented in Goethe's theory of metamorphosis a scientific method that aids research into life, into the *supraphysical* at work in the physical. The "archetypal plant" underlying all plants is not perceptible to the senses, but stands above the individual plant as creative idea.

It is this scientific method that now matters. The "archetypal plant" is not accessible to the ordinary intellectual powers. The intellect can register and systematize what lies physically before it in a fully developed state,★ at rest, finished, and therefore dead. The state of unrest, of becom-

---

★The German word for state is "Zustand," literally "to-stand," causing Goethe to say, "Zustand is a fatuous word, for nothing stands still, everything is in motion." (Niebuhr, November 23, 1812.)

ing instead of dying, the process, this the intellect cannot grasp. Quite different forces of perception are needed here. Goethe calls this soul force reason, the force that can grasp the living organism that is unrest in itself. He says:

> Reason depends on what is still becoming whereas the intellect depends on what has already become; the former cares not whither it is headed, the latter asks whence it has come. Reason finds joy in *developing*; the intellect seeks to preserve things for later use. (cf. Rudolf Steiner's introduction to Goethe's scientific writings.)

Thus, we have Goethe to thank for the perception that the organic nature can be understood only in its becoming, that is, in its development, and that for such an understanding a completely different kind of perceptive power is needed than conceptional, abstract thinking. I learn, to the extent that I train myself in Goethean thinking, to understand the temporal flow of life processes. I approach the general laws of transformation as they are outwardly expressed in the simplest organisms, the plants. What was once a mystery is now clear. Goethe called this mystery "the simplest thing you can think of," but bear in mind that it took him years to discover this simplest of all mysteries.

In this context, and as Goethe himself said, it is important to realize that the laws of metamorphosis extend to *all* living things. Hence, a theory of metamorphosis for animals and one for humans would also have to be possible. These would necessarily be considerably more complex than the one for plants, for unlike plants, the essential being of animals does not exhaust itself in growth and reproduction, since animals have a "real inner life." In addition to this inner life, however, the ego-endowed human being also has his individual destiny.

We must accept that Goethe's theory of metamorphosis alone is insufficient to understand the biography of an individual. It can, however, be considered a first step towards such understanding, for it acquaints us with metamorphoses in the organic world, and thus properly schools our thinking. But the path from theory of plant metamorphosis to theory of human metamorphosis must be sought elsewhere. It lies with Rudolf Steiner. His Anthroposophy can be experienced as an extension of Goethe's path of knowledge. Goethe leads us to the supraphysical in the elemental organic world; Rudolf Steiner goes farther to the supraphysical in human nature, and thereby to the knowledge of one's own biography as well as that of others. Anthroposophy encompasses a theory of human metamorphosis.

As we investigate the life and soul metamorphoses presented in Rudolf Steiner's Anthroposophy, as we inwardly recreate them by means of their outer, concrete manifestations, we experience a metamorphosis in ourselves; our thinking is transformed. The more we are transformed, the more we understand man as a being in the process of becoming. Dimly we foresee what kind of flower will spring from the seed. We uncover the hidden relationship between the specific capacity that blossoms in the adult and the seed unfolded in the child. We know what kind of seeds are necessary to produce beautiful flowers and good fruit. We can once again begin to believe in the educator in us! For does not education consist precisely in unfolding what lies as seed in the soul? Then, following its own laws without further help from us, the seed appears in later years as soul capacity and organic health. Through Rudolf Steiner's Anthroposophy we are steered toward education. He has made it possible for the teacher to educate properly out of the right insights.

To lay the groundwork for further remarks, I would now like to mention a life metamorphosis of the child, which although it has a great impact on education, develops out of the child's being in an elemental way and without adult intervention. It is a metamorphosis whose outer manifestations we have often witnessed with our own eyes.

By the time a child is seven or eight he has undergone a tremendous metamorphosis. But in order properly to appreciate what has been happening in the child according to nature's hidden laws, we must first know something about the infant. What does close observation of the infant reveal? Briefly and broadly, we see how he "sleeps away" most of the day, showing a relative wakefulness for only a few hours. Once awake, however, his existence consists almost entirely in kicking and wriggling, gurgling and screaming, eating and digesting. Whatever he does is triggered either by physical comfort or discomfort. Every move or sound he makes has an organic basis. Of a soul or spirit life there is no trace. Let us begin by asking the simple and totally nonacademic question, Where in the infant are the independent soul forces that emerge later?—Now, it is odd that we can have the deepest impressions precisely from such a small child. We feel immensely powerful forces at work in the child's organism. In comparison, the adult body seems to have almost none. This observation (and it is always a profound experience) can help us to answer our nonacademic question.

A wonderful capacity, which is still much too little understood, develops very early in the small child. It is the capacity to absorb everything happening, in the widest sense of the word, around him by imitating it. He absorbs it so thoroughly that it becomes woven into his own organism. The first things the small child picks up are the external characteristics of his environment that we can all see. For instance, he blinks his eyes like his father, he clears his throat slightly before speaking just like his mother, he makes the same gestures with his hands that she does, he starts to walk as he does. So much of what is attributed to heredity is nothing more than imitation. We just don't see it because we equate the child's elemental imitative force with the adult's ability to imitate any number of things, when in fact, as I hope to show, there is quite a principal difference. We find the remnants of the child's imitative force in the actor, comedian and clown. It is the natural physical basis of artistic genius.

The small child can adopt the adult's infirmities and organic disorders by imitation. He can imitate himself into a little asthmatic, for example, who can only be cured with medication, so deeply is "it" imbedded in the body already. Why is that possible? Because the child is using *organic* forces to imitate, not soul forces. The imitative force of the small child is not the manifestation of a pure soul force, but the expression of a life force at work in the organs. According to Rudolf Steiner, the entire body is given to the environment in religious surrender, be the environment good or bad.

The child, however, does not only adopt external characteristics. He also absorbs less tangible things, such as the adult's thoughts and feelings, and uses them to form his organs. Rudolf Steiner said, "Our thoughts live on in the physical body of the child." Later, they appear as a strength or weakness of the *organs*. A time will come, Rudolf Steiner goes on to say, when prospective doctors, educators and psychologists will choose quite different themes for their dissertations than they do today. They might, for example, discuss the following situation: At the age of forty-eight a man succumbs to an illness with such and such symptoms. The illness is found to stem from certain ugly thoughts that confronted the subject as a child of four or five. (cf. Rudolf Steiner, *The Roots of Education*.) It will behoove future biographers as well to adopt the basic attitude and insight expressed in this kind of dissertation theme.

Close observation of the child's imitative power shows

clearly enough that it is not yet a capacity of the soul, but one of the body. Well then, what about the memory, which, in a certain form at least, can come to light quite early? Again, very exact observation reveals that until the age of seven the "memory" undergoes various stages of development, emerging as an independent *soul* capacity only around the seventh year. The farther back we go, the more transformed appears that which from a certain point on we may call "memory."

We adults learn through the memory, and it takes us both time and special inner effort to turn this memory into ability. The extent to which this can be done even becomes a matter of destiny. With the small child there is a principal difference in the learning process. Not that he learns less in the first three years of his life than an adult during the same timespan. On the contrary, the small child learns much more by far. He learns to stand up, to walk and talk, to sit at the table, to eat with a spoon, to drink a glass of milk without spilling a drop. He learns to dress himself, tie his shoes, wash his hands and comb his hair. He learns thousands of things that require extraordinary dexterity. It is precisely in these few examples, however, that we see in what the child's learning consists. Far from being memorized knowledge it is a skill, an ability right from the start, for the child's "memory," like his imitative principle, has an organic or bodily rather than a soul basis. Everything that the child does over and over with his body, "but in his body's innermost being," then becomes memory. It is not memory in the adult sense, however, but "automatic behavior," as Rudolf Steiner once called it. In the adult all impressions first dwell in the realm of the soul as memory. In the child they want to become immediate skills. Only gradually, passing through various stages of development, is this automatic behavior transformed into the capacity that can then justly be called memory.

I have in this way already hinted at the tremendous metamorphosis that culminates after the seventh or eighth year. How the child's being has changed! No longer does he live through his limbs, through gestures. Now he likes "dancing," playing team sports, singing songs, and trying a new instrument. He has, generally speaking, an instinctive relationship to rhythm and music. The powers of memory now live in him, resting in themselves, as a free activity of the soul. An elemental and pictorial thinking now gives him an affinity for the fairy tales, fables and myths related to it. His relationship to his environment, especially to adults, has completely changed. He no longer wants to model his *organs* on his environment—instead, he seeks to model his *soul* on what the adult, whom he yearns to respect as an authority, reveals to him. We can well say that his relationships to adults now have a soul rather than an organic basis.

Now the moment has come when we must return to the nonacademic (but by no means unscientific) question posed earlier: Where does the power of memory come from? Where does elemental thinking originate? These powers seem nonexistent in the small child, yet they cannot have been conjured up out of thin air. Goethe can help us understand Rudolf Steiner's response to this question. Let us recall Goethe's words on organic nature: It can be comprehended only in its becoming—not with the intellect, which comprehends only what has come to rest, but with reason (a qualitatively different kind of thinking). Through Goethe's theory of metamorphosis we understand how in organic nature one thing develops out of another, not according to an external mechanical principle (as with man-made machines), but according to an inner, higher principle that governs all phenomena of organic nature. By means of constant, invisible changes, one and the same supraphysical basic force appears first as plant seed, then as stem, leaf, flower, fruit and new seed. If, by inwardly experiencing such real metamorphoses, we make our thinking alive, thereby schooling it methodically in the proper way, for the plant itself provides the proper method for researching the organic world, then the intellectual power and life force needed to understand the complex life and soul metamorphoses in man grow in us, and we can "see" for ourselves what Rudolf Steiner said about them. Their inner truth becomes quite clear to us. Physical proof is then no more necessary than proof that a fish is a fish and not a stone that has fun swimming around in the water.

What does Rudolf Steiner say to our eminently important scientific question? Out of his perceptions concerning the being of man he demonstrates how all supraphysical forces are still purely organic forces in the infant, devoted entirely to his physical body. All his forces are enmeshed with the physical body, serving it alone. With the small child, as with the plant, the "entelechy" appears as the formative force of the individual organs.

Rudolf Steiner shows us how these purely formative forces undergo an invisible change, reemerging at the age of seven as pure soul forces, as memory, as thinking. The same supraphysical basic force appears first as organ-forming force and then as memory. Growth forces metamorphose into thinking forces. If we have wondered, Why can't the small child think? we can now answer, Because the child still needs the "thinking forces" to digest milk, for example.

This organ force has created form even in hard stone. The permanent teeth are both the granite *memorials* of such creative forming and the keystones of a developmental phase, for now the forces used to form teeth can be used to form thoughts. For the educator, much depends on whether or not he can comprehend "the hidden kinship" between the teeth and thinking. Experiencing the teeth as the image of thinking in nature is a meditation exercise for the teacher.

The transformation of growth forces into thinking forces can perhaps be called an *elemental* metamorphosis, because it is a completely internal and natural occurrence, in which no other human being is involved. The life of the child continues in this kind of what I would like to call elemental metamorphoses, and the teacher must orient himself accordingly. In addition, however, there are other kinds of life and soul metamorphoses, namely those which the teacher himself calls forth in the child. Every act of the teacher undergoes hidden transformations in the child, reappearing years later in such changed form that only life-comprehending reason can recognize it. To the mere intellect it must remain hidden.

One of these metamorphoses moves in reverse compared with those described earlier. Where once the organ-forming force was transformed into soul capacity, now the opposite is true as soul force is changed into organic form.

Though we can speak of sovereign soul capacities in the school child, keen observation nevertheless reveals that the interaction of body and soul is still very close. There is no sign at all of the schism that we find in adults. This makes the most diverse transformations from soul forces to organic forces possible, the one easily slipping into the other.

To illustrate what has just been said consider the following example: At thirty-eight an individual experiences some kind of anomalies in his soul life, a "neurosis." The Freudian says to himself, There is a knot, a "complex" in the soul of this man, in his "subconscious"; it leads an uncontrolled, separate existence, and is now even beginning to rumble. It is this rumbling that is making the patient neurotic. The troublemaker must be tracked down, grabbed by the hair and rendered harmless. Using his highly developed intellectual feelers, the psychoanalyst dives into the patient's subconscious and systematically searches for the troublesome complex. This work is not unlike that of the deep-sea diver exploring the ocean floor. Experience (the analyst's!) usually proves the complex to be a childhood trauma. By raising the complex, which until now has been rumbling in the depths of the soul, to the surface of the consciousness, the experts believe the soul disturbance can be removed.

In a question-and-answer period Rudolf Steiner addressed this precise issue. "Every soul trauma," he said, "also has an organic effect, especially in children. Everything that happens to the soul has corresponding physical repercussions that alter the course of the organism's development. After a very specific number of years (life passes rhythmically), and as a result of these repercussions, a repetition of the initial effect on the organs occurs. The retraumatized organs now act back on the soul, which is traumatized in turn. Therefore, instead of analyzing the patient's subconscious we should be examining his physical health." (cf. "Bemerkungen zur Psychoanalyse," *Die Menschenschule,* IV, 1930, pp. 197.)

Two very different and opposing methods of observing people confront us here. In the Freudian view of people a cleverly trained intellect is at work. But this intellectual perception can see only what has already become, what no longer contains any life. Therefore, Freud must consider the ever new transformations of the truly alive in the sensory world also as having come to rest, as being dead. His intellect prevents him from following the transformations of man's "unconscious." Overcoming that block would require a Goethean transformation of his thinking. In order to experience inwardly what is still becoming form, he would have to develop the capacity of reason, still Goethean, in himself. Failure to do this has made Freudian psychoanalysis what it is today, containing theories such as this: A traumatic soul experience lies in the depths of the soul like a heavy, lifeless stone. Simply its heaviness and dead existence allow

it to rumble at certain times. No thinking is more un-Goethean
than Freud's!

Rudolf Steiner expands Goethe's theory of metamorphosis
to include a science of human metamorphosis. It embraces
the processes of becoming in man, that which is unrest in itself. Rudolf Steiner can thus show, to remain with the same
example, how the soul transformed by trauma penetrates
the most delicate organic processes and continues to work as
an organic force. Rather than stopping there, however, it
works on, and after a certain interval it seeks to revert to a
soul force. These are significant metamorphoses for the
teacher, and he does well to remain conscious of them. He
must now say to himself, If everything that a child experiences with his soul affects the growth, circulation and diges-
tion processes, then it no longer makes sense to consider
teaching merely as the education of soul and spirit; for then
everything I do to strengthen the child in soul and spirit also
involves organic strengthening, and if I mistreat the soul of
the child through improper education, then this mistreat-
ment will manifest itself as an organic weakness. (Note that
the external effect of this organic strengthening or weaken-
ing becomes visible only many years later as physical health
or illness.) Therefore, said Rudolf Steiner, proper education
of the mind and spirit is also the best physical education.

Today's educational methods cultivate the mind of the
child as though there were no physical side, and when—in
physical education classes—it is the body's turn to be trained,
the soul is not considered relevant. Why? Because the usual
thinking cannot recognize the transformations of bodily into
soul forces and vice-versa.

Once we have developed a certain talent for observation
we can see things happening in the children during the
lesson that we missed before. If we succeed, for example, in
structuring the lesson truly according to the child's needs,

in other words "artistically," then we can see how pleasantly flushed the children's faces become. Even normally very pale faces acquire a healthy red glow. We also discover that the children are breathing more freely and lightly, but nevertheless more intensely than usual. If, however, despite all our wonderful pedagogical knowledge, we have taught all morning as a fossilized schoolmaster, merely out of our highly developed intellect, then, provided our eyes have become sharp enough, we can read the effects of such teaching in the children. We see that their faces are somewhat paler, somewhat more drained of blood than usual, even if only slightly; or we may suddenly notice that the children no longer breathe as freely as before. It may appear that their breathing has become somewhat oppressed. These phenomena can be interpreted only as the most blatant effects of extremely delicate organic processes. The phenomena disappear soon enough, but the effects of the organic processes remain behind. Through these observations we learn that many illnesses—such as weak lungs, poor circulation, premature sclerosis—that emerge in later years must be rooted in improper education.

Here, dissertation topics for future doctors, psychologists and educators abound. Future biographers must also be expected to possess a living knowledge of such metamorphoses. More important still for the educator, however, is the truly shocking realization that, for better or for worse, he largely co-determines the "biography" of the children entrusted to him.

Although all soul forces awakened in the child by the teacher call forth attendant organic processes, it would obviously be wrong to imagine that these soul forces are converted in their entirety into organic ones. If that were the case, then all education of the soul and spirit would effectively be mere physical education. True, each stimulation to the child's soul triggers fine changes in the organic processes, but the soul remains sovereign and is transformed according to its own inherent laws.

Proper education continuously unfolds dormant soul forces in the child. They are "soul seeds," which awaken only in later years. Why can they awaken, grow and bloom? Because the child, rather than being finished or closed off like the adult, is still in the process of becoming. The practice of considering the child merely as an organism in space is unproductive for education. Whoever cannot see the child also as an organism in time should not be involved in education. Unlike the adult, the child as such is nothing but a giant seed. Rudolf Steiner called him an "adult in seed form." If man were born as an adult, as a (relatively speaking) "finished product," then he could no longer be educated; his destiny would be fixed and his life would unfold automatically. Fortunately, man is born unfinished in every way, so that education can help transform destiny into freedom.

In contrast, let us take a cursory look at the young animal. It is not an "adult in seed form," but a being that cannot become a full-grown, fully developed animal fast enough. Because it rashly makes this immediate leap into maturity in one fell swoop, the animal loses the opportunity to be educated, to become a human being. (cf. Poppelbaum, *Mensch und Tier*. Rud Geering, Basel 1928.)

Everything we try to unfold in the child, this "adult in seed form," must therefore not be something finished, but must itself be seminal, capable of development. But what happens when we make the child absorb finished concepts and abstractions the way adults do? Then we force him to use his intellectual forces all at once instead of unfolding them gradually. We cut him off from the chance to develop, and thus from the chance to become a "man." Instead of making a man of him we turn him into an intellectual animal.

If, however, we succeed in unfolding living "soul seeds" in the child, then they will grow along with the child, undergoing hidden, secret changes, and years later they will burst into bloom. How different the blossom often is from the seed! So many times the seed gives birth to a force that seems its complete opposite, making it difficult to discover the hidden relationship. It cannot be pinpointed by psychoanalysis, and it does not register on experimental psychology's most sophisticated devices. The truth is revealed to him who schools his thinking first on Goethe and then on Rudolf Steiner.

The following are examples of pure soul metamorphoses that Rudolf Steiner has brought to our attention.

At around the age of seven (the first signs appear much earlier, of course) the child displays a first elementary thinking. Still very different from adult thinking, it is closer to the pictorial thinking we find in the fairy tales and myths of all nations, which is why children love those stories so much. But people often have reservations about telling fairy tales. Some wonder whether the child who hears so many fairy tales won't become a dreamer, unable later on to distinguish between dream and reality. With the proper insight into the child's soul and its metamorphoses we can answer as follows: By using education to cultivate the child's pictorial thinking (the most natural thing in the world), and that means not only through fairy tales, but through all our teaching, we plant seeds that grow into healthy adult thinking; they become completely realistic thinking, which is rationality itself, and which cannot be intoxicated or deceived by any kind of phantastic ideas. Pictorial, imaginative thinking, tended properly and with care, will in due course be transformed into rational, clear thinking.

A second example: Only around fifteen is the child mature enough to arrive at a personal judgment; only then can he grasp causal connections intellectually. Between seven and fourteen it is natural for him to want to abstain from thinking and judging on his own. He wants to use the adult as a yardstick against which to measure the world. He seeks to shape his soul in the *adult's* image. What the adult imagines as good, beautiful and true the child accepts as such. We can experience how the child (unconsciously, of course) wants no part of thinking on his own, of inner independence, of the freedom to make his own judgments, preferring instead to develop in himself feelings of respect, and indeed of authority.—What becomes of these soul seeds of respect and authority? They are transformed, reappearing in later years as the ability to use freedom properly, to think, feel and act out of one's own individuality! They reveal themselves as the basis of the well-centered force of personality. How do we raise free men? By developing feelings of respect and natural—not forcibly instilled—authority in the child! How do we "raise" unfree men, completely lacking in independent thinking? By triggering the force of judgment as early as possible in the child, in order to reach in *one* leap what can come only as the goal of a long development.

A further example: There are individuals who do not seem any smarter, stronger willed or more successful than others, and yet people speak of them with a very special admiration. Many seek out these individuals for advice, driven by distress and anguish. What kind of force emanates from such a man (who may even live in the most modest circumstances)? In his presence we are somehow protected from all evil within and around us. A protective force flows from him. It endures long after we have left his presence, and contains healing powers. At the risk of sounding old-fashioned, I feel compelled to say that blessed forces stream from such a person. When we have this experience, we may well ask ourselves where such a strong soul force comes from. The answer, which can be found through Rudolf Steiner, is that as a child this man or woman learned to pray in the right way. Perhaps the following will shed some light on this soul metamorphosis: When we allow a child to pray out of the right attitude of heart, we cause him to give himself trustingly into the care of divine spiritual beings, to let himself be protected and blessed by them; and this ability to receive blessing is transformed into the power to bless others.

One last example: Based on the recognition, correct in and of itself, that the child is not an adult, an educational method has arisen in recent years that is intent on treating the child strictly as a child. Practitioners of this method withhold from the child anything that he cannot fully understand at that fleeting stage of his development. They believe that a soul need of the child is being fulfilled this way, using the analogy that the adult, too, wishes to understand everything fully, to the point where he feels quite uncomfortable if understanding something takes a little longer than he would like.

This teaching trend is unnatural and, therefore, unpedagogical. It is true that the child is not a smaller, less knowledgeable adult. Yet neither is he a nearly finished adult, who can absorb any missing knowledge like an adult. Nor is he a being who wants to remain a child forever. Both cases present a false picture of the child's being. On the one hand we have the nearly complete adult, on the other, the complete child. Both ways of looking at the situation express the inability to see the child as a temporal organism, as an "adult in seed form," i.e. that he wants to mature into an adult in soul and spirit.

The described teaching trend thus tends to offer the child nothing beyond his own horizon, which is very narrowly defined in the first place. The child is condemned to live in an uninspiring, restricted world, where nothing can overtax his powers of comprehension. Many primers and readers are assembled along these lines. Poems are also selected very carefully to avoid any thought leading away from the commonplace into world expanses and thought depths. Not the slightest hint must be dropped in the child's presence that great truths exist which cannot be won without struggle.

On the other hand, what happens in the child's soul if we allow him to absorb great and deep truths purely by memory, since he cannot yet understand them with his intellect? Let us try to understand the process properly. Through his memory the child takes something into his soul that he cannot grasp with his intellect. Setting aside understanding, he absorbs it nonetheless. This abandoned acceptance of something still unfathomable, something barely glimpsed by the soul, becomes a seed, grows, and is transformed. What does it turn into? It becomes the force to understand the most profound and ultimate truths, but now with the "entire man" (or, as Troxler would say, with the heart). What is absorbed by the memory in this way is transformed into strong forces of perception!

The fear of memorization is thus unfounded. I hasten to add, however, that the truths we give the child to memorize must be truly profound ones. For example, the beginning of the Gospel according to St. John or the beginning of the story of Creation, a myth, a fairy tale. The "profound truths" come in many forms. Nothing else can become a seed, and thus cannot be transformed into a force of perception. The most it can do is present a great obstacle for this force. Highest truths, however, taken into the child's soul by memorization, are transformed into highest human forces of perception.

Such truths as those mentioned above create a new method of education. Without them we cannot educate, nor understand biographies, nor know ourselves. Such truths, absorbed in a living way, are a path towards self-knowledge.

Footnotes

[1]Rudolf Steiner, *The Philosophy of Freedom*, trans. Michael Wilson (London: Rudolf Steiner Press, 1970), pp. 138, 140, 142.

[2]Johann Heinrich Pestalozzi, *How Gertrude Teaches her Children*, trans. Lucy E. Holland and Francis C. Turner (London: Remax House, 1966), p. 178.

Translator's note in above reference: "The Heidelberg or Palatinate Catechism was compiled and published by the Heidelberg theologians Zacharias Ursinus and Kaspar Olevianaus in 1553 by command and with the cooperation of Prince Elector Friedrich III of the Palatinate. It was and is the most popular elementary book of religious instruction in the schools of the Swiss Evangelical Confession. The little book has a preponderant doctrinal character, and was therefore not suited for Pestalozzi's teaching."

[3]Translator's note: All German nouns are capitalized.

[4]Translator's note: An ell (*ulna* in Latin), is a former measure, of different lengths in different countries, used chiefly for measuring cloth. The English ell was forty-five inches. The Flemish ell was twenty-seven inches or three-quarters of a yard.

[5]Friedrich Nietzsche, *Untimely Meditations*, trans. R.J. Hollingdale (Cambridge, England: Cambridge University Press, 1983), p. 78.

[6]Ibid., p. 86.

[7]Ibid., p. 120.

[8]Ibid., p. 63.

[9]Ibid., p. 80.

[10]Ibid., p. 121.

[11]Rudolf Steiner, *The Philosophy of Freedom*, trans. Michael Wilson (London: Rudolf Steiner Press, 1970), pp. 32, 33, 42, 43.

[12]Rudolf Steiner, *Knowledge of the Higher Worlds and its Attainment*, trans. G. Metaxa (Bell's Pond, Hudson, New York, Anthroposophic Press, 1985), p. 7.

[13]Nietzsche, *Untimely Meditations*, p. 94.

[14]Johann Wolfgang von Goethe, *Faust II* (New York: Random House,

Modern Library Edition, 1950), p. 72.

[15]Nietzsche, *Untimely Meditations*, p. 78.

[16]Ibid., p. 84.

[17]Ibid., p. 80.

[18]Ibid., p. 121.

[19]Ibid., p. 94.

[20]T.R. Sethna, *The Teachings of Zarathustra, the Prophet of Iran, on How to Think and Succeed in Life* (Karachi, Pakistan: Times Subscription Agency, NADIR House, 1966), p. 28.

[21]Edmond Bordeaux Szekely, *The World Picture of Zarathustra* (Tecate, California: Essene School, 1953), p. 61.

[22]Ibid., p. 62.

[23]Ibid., p. 122.

[24]Nietzsche, *Untimely Meditations*, p. 62.

[25]Ibid., p. 115.

Bibliography

1. Books by Rudolf Steiner

Balance in Teaching. 2nd ed. Spring Valley, NY: Mercury Press, 1982. 58 pages.

Deeper Insights in Education: The Waldorf Approach. Trans. Rene Querido. Spring Valley, NY: Anthroposophic Press, 1983. 63 pages.

Discussions with Teachers. Trans. Helen Fox. London: Rudolf Steiner Press, 1967. 168 pages.

Education as a Social Problem. Trans. Lisa D. Monges and Doris M. Bugbey. Spring Valley, NY: Anthroposophic Press, 1969. 115 pages.

Education as an Art. Ed. Paul M. Allen. Trans. Michael Tapp and Elisabeth Tapp. Blauvelt, NY: Steinerbooks, Garber Communications, 1970. 126 pages.

The Education of the Child in the Light of Anthroposophy. Trans. Mary Adams and George Adams. 2nd ed. London: Rudolf Steiner Press, 1975.

Essentials of Education. Trans. Jesse Darrell. 2nd ed. London: Rudolf Steiner Press, 1968. 95 pages.

The Four Temperaments. Trans. Frances E. Dawson. 2nd ed. Spring Valley, NY: Anthroposophic Press, 1976. 59 pages.

Human Values in Education. Trans. Vera Compton-Burnett. London: Rudolf Steiner Press, 1971. 190 pages.

The Kingdom of Childhood. Trans. Helen Fox. London: Rudolf Steiner Press, 1964. 165 pages.

Lectures to Teachers. Trans. Daphne Harwood. 2nd ed. London: Anthroposophical Publishing Company, 1931. 95 pages.

A Modern Art of Education. Trans. Jesse Darrell and George Adams. 3rd ed. London: Rudolf Steiner Press, 1954. 232 pages.

Practical Advice to Teachers. Trans. Johanna Collis. 2nd ed. London: Rudolf Steiner Press, 1976. 206 pages.

Prayers for Mothers and Children. Trans. Eileen V. Hersey and Christian von Arnim. 3rd ed. London: Rudolf Steiner Press, 1983. 78 pages.

The Renewal of Education through the Science of the Spirit. Trans. Roland Everett. Bournemouth, England: Kolisko Archive, for Steiner Schools Fellowship, 1981. 217 pages.

The Roots of Education. Trans. Helen Fox. London: Rudolf Steiner Press, 1968. 95 pages.

A Social Basis for Primary and Secondary Education. Forest Row, England: Michael Hall School, 1958, mimeographed. 43 pages.

The Spiritual Ground of Education. Trans. Daphne Harwood. London: Anthroposophical Publishing Company, 1947. 136 pages.

Study of Man: General Education Course. A.C. Harwood. 2nd ed. London: Rudolf Steiner Press, 1966. 191 pages.

Three Lectures for Teachers. Forest Row, England: Steiner Schools Fellowship, n.d., mimeographed. 25 pages.

Waldorf Education for Adolescence. Bournemouth, England: Kolisko Archive, for Steiner Schools Fellowship, 1980. 107 pages.

2. *General Treatments by Other Authors*

Aeppli, Willi. *The Care and Development of the Human Senses.* Trans. Valerie Freilich. Forest Row, England: Steiner Schools Fellowship, n.d. 84 pages.

Baravalle, Hermann von. *The International Waldorf School Movement.* Spring Valley, NY: Waldorf School Monographs, St. George Book Service, 1960. 50 pages.

Carlgren, Frans. *Education towards Freedom.* Ed. Joan Rudel and Siegfried Rudel. East Grinstead, England: Lanthorn Press, 1981. 208 pages.

Easton, Stewart C. "The New Art of Education. The Waldorf School Movement" in *Man and World in the Light of Anthroposophy.* 2nd ed. Spring Valley, NY: Anthroposophic Press, 1982. Pp. 382–411.

Edmunds, Francis. *Rudolf Steiner Education: The Waldorf Schools.* London: Rudolf Steiner Press, 1979. 134 pages.

Harwood, A. C(ecil). *The Recovery of Man in Childhood: A Study in the Educational Work of Rudolf Steiner.* Spring Valley, NY: Anthroposophic Press, 1981, 1958. 208 pages.

_____, *The Way of a Child: An Introduction to the Work of Rudolf Steiner for Children.* London: Rudolf Steiner Press, 1967. 144 pages.

Heydebrand, Caroline von, comp. *The Curriculum of the First Waldorf School.* Ed. with additions Eileen Hutchins. Forest Row, England: Steiner Schools Fellowship, 1966. 75 pages.

Holtzapfel, Walter. *Children's Destinies: The Three Directions of Man's Development.* Trans. Madge Childs. 2nd ed. Spring Valley, NY: Mercury Press, 1984. 90 pages.

Howard, Alan. *You Wanted to Know . . . What a Waldorf School Is . . .*

And What It Is Not. Spring Valley, NY: St. George Publications, 1983. 53 pages.

Jarman, Ron, ed. *Child and Man Extracts.* Forest Row, England: Steiner Schools Fellowship, 1975. 435 pages.

Lissau, Magda. *The Temperaments and the Arts: Their Relation and Function in Waldorf Pedagogy.* Chicago: Magda Lissau, 1983; Distributed by St. George Book Service, Spring Valley, NY. 135 pages.

Lyons, Nick and Piening, Ekkehard, eds. *Educating as an Art. Essays on The Rudolf Steiner Method—Waldorf Education.* New York: Rudolf Steiner School Press, 1979; Distributed by Anthoposophic Press, Spring Valley, NY. 183 pages.

Querido, Rene. *Creativity in Education.* San Francisco: Dakin, 1982. 77 pages.

Richards, M(ary). C(aroline). *Toward Wholeness: Rudolf Steiner Education in America.* Middletown, CT: Wesleyan University Press, 1980. 210 pages.

Rist, Georg and Schneider, Peter. *Integrating Vocational and General Education: A Rudolf Steiner School.* Hamburg, West Germany: UNESCO Institute for Education, 1979; Distributed by Unipub, Ann Arbor, MI. 196 pages.

Stockmeyer, E.A. Karl. *Rudolf Steiner's Curriculum for Waldorf Schools.* Trans. R. Everett-Zade. Forest Row, England: Steiner Schools Fellowship, 1982. 240 pages.

Wilkinson, Roy. *Commonsense Schooling.* East Grinstead, England: Henry Goulden, 1978. 98 pages.

_____. *The Curriculum of the Rudolf Steiner School.* Forest Row, England: Roy Wilkinson, 1982. 29 pages.

_____. *Questions and Answers on Rudolf Steiner Education.* East Grinstead, England. Henry Goulden, 1980. 33 pages.

3. *On Specific Subjects by Other Authors*

Baravalle, Hermann von. *Astronomy: An Introduction.* Spring Valley, NY: Waldorf School Monographs, St. George Book Service, 1974. 40 pages.

_____. *Geometric Drawing and the Waldorf School Plan.* Spring Valley, NY: Waldorf School Monographs, St. George Book Service, 1967. 56 pages.

_____. *Introduction to Physics in the Waldorf Schools.* Spring Valley, NY: Waldorf School Monographs, St. George Book Service, 1962. 41 pages.

_____. *Perspective Drawing.* Spring Valley, NY: Waldorf School Monographs, St. George Book Service, 1960. 46 pages.

_____. *The Teaching of Arithmetic and the Waldorf School Plan.* Spring Valley, NY: Waldorf School Monographs, St. George Book Service, 1967. 40 pages.

Frohlich, Margaret and Niederhauser, Hans. *Form Drawing.* Spring Valley, NY: Mercury Press, 1984. 57 pages.

Gabert, Erich. *Punishment in Self-Education and in the Education of the Child.* Trans. Pauline Wehrle. Forest Row, England: Steiner Schools Fellowship, n.d. 52 pages.

Glas, Werner. *The Waldorf School Approach to History.* Spring Valley, NY: Anthroposophic Press, 1981. 102 pages.

Gorge, Alice A. *Creative Toymaking.* 2nd ed. Edinburgh, Great Britain: Floris Books, 1981. 58 pages.

Grahl, Ursula. *The Wisdom in Fairy Tales.* East Grinstead, England: New Knowledge Books, 1969. 43 pages.

Hahn, Herbert. *From the Wellsprings of the Soul: Towards the Religious Teaching of the Young.* Trans. Anne Barnes. Forest Row, England: Steiner Schools Fellowship, 1977. 107 pages.

Hauck, Hedwig. *Handwork and Handicrafts from Indications by Rudolf Steiner, Part 1.* Trans. Graham Rickett. Forest Row, England: Steiner Schools Fellowship, 1968. 101 pages.

Jaffke, Freya. *Making Soft Toys.* Trans. Rosemary Gebert. Edinburgh, Great Britain: Floris Books, 1981. 59 pages.

Kolisko, Eugen. *Elementary Chemistry: Combustion, Lime, Salt, Water, Metals.* Bournemouth, England: Kolisko Archive, 1978. 30 pages.

_____. *Geology.* Bournemouth, England: Kolisko Archive, 1979. 18 pages.

_____. *Natural History.* Bournemouth, England: Kolisko Archive, 1979. 22 pages.

McAllen, Audrey. *Teaching Children to Write: Its Connection with the Development of Spatial Consciousness.* London: Rudolf Steiner Press, 1977. 80 pages.

_____. *The Extra Lesson: Exercises in Movement, Drawing and Painting for Helping Children in Difficulties with Writing, Reading and Arithmetic.* London: Audrey McAllen, 1974. 78 pages.

Strauss, Michaela. *Understanding Children's Drawings.* London: Rudolf Steiner Press, 1978. 95 pages.

Wilkinson, Roy. A series of booklets on teaching many individual subjects, such as *Teaching History* (4 vols.), *Teaching Mathematics,*

Teaching English, Teaching Geography, The Interpretation of Fairy Tales, etc.) Forest Row, England: Roy Wilkinson.

4. *For Parents*

Carey, Diana and Large, Judy. *Festivals, Family and Food.* Stroud, England: Hawthorne Press, 1982. 223 pages.

Cusick, Lois. *Waldorf Parenting Handbook: Useful Information on Child Development and Education from Anthroposophical Sources.* 2nd ed. Spring Valley, NY: St. George Publications, 1984. 160 pages.

Glas, Norbert. *Conception, Birth and Early Childhood.* Spring Valley, NY: Anthroposophic Press, 1983. 154 pages.

Davy, Gudrun and Voors, Bons, eds. *Lifeways: Working with Family Questions.* Stroud, England: Hawthorne Press, 1983. 216 pages.

König, Karl. *Brothers and Sisters: The Order of Birth in the Family.* Spring Valley, NY: Anthroposophic Press and Edinburgh, Great Britain: Floris Books, 1984. 91 pages.

————. *The First Three Years of the Child.* Spring Valley, NY: Anthroposophic Press and Edinburgh, Great Britain: Floris Books, 1983. 136 pages.

Large Martin. *Who's Bringing Them Up? Television and Child Development.* Stroud, England: Hawthorne Press, 1980. 136 pages.

Linden, Wilhelm zur. *A Child Is Born: Pregnancy, Birth, Early Childhood.* London: Rudolf Steiner Press, 1980. 223 pages.

Sleigh, Julian. *Thirteen to Nineteen: Growing Frèe.* Edinburgh, Great Britain: Floris Books, 1982. 32 pages.

Smith, Susan. *Echoes of a Dream: Creative Beginnings for Parent and Child.* London, Canada: Waldorf School Association of London, 1982. 68 pages.

BASIC BOOKS

Rudolf Steiner intended these carefully written volumes to serve as a foundation and introduction to all of the later, more advanced anthroposophical writings and lecture courses.

THEOSOPHY, AN INTRODUCTION TO THE SUPER-SENSIBLE KNOWLEDGE OF THE WORLD AND THE DESTINATION OF MAN
by Rudolf Steiner

In this work Steiner carefully explains many of the basic concepts and terminologies of anthroposophy. The book begins with a sensitive description of the fundamental trichotomy: body, soul, and spirit, elaborating the various higher members of the human constitution. A discussion of reincarnation and karma follows. The next and longest chapter (75 pages) presents, in a vast panorama, the seven regions of the soul world, the seven regions of the land of spirits, and the soul's journey after death through these worlds. A brief discussion of the path to higher knowledge follows.

"Read . . . Rudolf Steiner's little book on theosophy—your hair will stand on end!" Saul Bellow in **Newsweek**

(395 pp)   0-91014-239-4 Paper
                                            0-91014-265-3 Cloth

AN OUTLINE OF OCCULT SCIENCE *by Rudolf Steiner*

This lengthy work begins with a thorough discussion and definition of the term "occult" science. A description of the supersensible nature of the human being follows, along with a discussion of dreams, sleep, death, life between death and rebirth, and reincarnation. In the fourth chapter evolution is described from the perspective of initiation science. The fifth chapter characterizes the training a student must undertake as a preparation for initiation. The sixth and seventh chapters consider the future evolution of the world and more detailed observations regarding supersensible realities.

(388 pp)   0-91014-275-0 Paper
                                            0-91014-226-2 Cloth

CHRISTIANITY AS MYSTICAL FACT *by Rudolf Steiner*

This early fundamental work, written in 1902 enlarged in 1910, seeks to show how Christianity arose out of what was prepared in the pre-Christian Mysteries. Christianity, however, was not merely a further development of what existed in these Mysteries but something unique and independent, arising much in the same way that a seed arises out of the soil. Included are chapters on: The Mysteries and Mystery Wisdom, The Greek Sages Before Plato, Plato as a Mystic, Mystery Wisdom of Egypt, Steiner then goes on to consider: The Gospels, The Lazarus Miracle, The Apocalypse of St. John, Jesus and His Historical Background, The Nature of Christianity, Christianity and Pagan Wisdom, and St. Augustine and the Church. This book is a foundation for what Steiner later more fully develops concerning the nature of Christ and Christianity. Also published in a different translation as *Christianity and Occult Mysteries of Antiquity.*

(195 pp)   0-88010-159-8 Paper

KNOWLEDGE OF THE HIGHER WORLDS AND ITS ATTAINMENT *by Rudolf Steiner*

Rudolf Steiner's fundamental work on the path to higher knowledge explains in detail the exercises and disciplines a student must pursue in order to attain a wakeful experience of supersensible realities. The stages of Preparation, Enlightenment, and Initiation are described, as are the transformation of dream life and the meeting with the Guardian of the Threshold. Moral exercises for developing each of the spiritual lotus petal organs ("chakras") are given in accordance with the rule of taking three steps in moral development for each step into spiritual knowledge. The path described here is a safe one which will not interfere with the student's ability to lead a normal outer life.

(237 pp)   0-88010-046-X Paper
                                            0-88010-045-1 Cloth

THE PHILOSOPHY OF SPIRITUAL ACTIVITY *by Rudolf Steiner*

Translated by William Lindeman. "Is human action free?" asks Steiner in his most important philosophical work. By first addressing the nature of knowledge, Steiner cuts across the ancient debate of real or illusory human freedom. A painstaking examination of human experience as a polarity of percepts and concepts shows that only in thinking does one escape the compulsion of natural law. Steiner's argument arrives at the recognition of the self-sustaining, universal reality of thinking that embraces both subjective and objective validity. Free acts can be performed out of love for a "moral intuition" grasped ever anew by a living thinking activity. Steiner scrutinizes numerous world-views and philosophical positions and indicates the relevance of his conclusions to human relations and life's ultimate questions. As he later pointed out, the sequence of thoughts in this book can also become a path toward spiritual knowledge.

(284 pp)   0-88010-156-3 Paper
                                            0-88010-157-1 Cloth

On Child Development and Waldorf Education

THE RECOVERY OF MAN IN CHILDHOOD *by A.C. Harwood*

Piaget and other modern child development researchers attempt to study the emergence of adult capacities in the child. But, as A.C. Harwood points out in this absorbing study of Rudolf Steiner's educational work, childhood is a time of *losing*, as well as gaining, capacities. Is there a connection between the loss of a child's faculty and the acquisition of an adult one? Yes, answers Harwood—in fact, a threefold connection.

There follows an insightful survey of the three seven-year stages of child development as depicted by Steiner. This is presented in connection with numerous examples and anecdotes on Waldorf education's use of curriculum subjects to support and assist this developmental child-man exchange. Other chapters take up specific facets of Waldorf education, such as foreign languages, eurythmy and music, and the temperaments. These lucid and literate explanations qualify this book as the most intelligent and stimulating introductory work on that unique approach to educating known often as "education as an art."

(211 pp)   0-88010-001-X Paper

TEACHING AS A LIVELY ART *by Marjorie Spock*
The author systematically describes the stages of a child's development from 6 to 13 years of age. The education methods appropriate to these different periods are discussed. There are also chapters on the temperaments, the teacher, and the relation between teacher and child.

(138 pp)   0-88010-127-X Paper

THE WALDORF SCHOOL APPROACH TO HISTORY *by Werner Glas, Ph.D.*
This important work is addressed to parents, teachers, and the general reader interested in education. It is based on ideas which have been put to the test in the classrooms of the rapidly expanding Waldorf School movement. Chapter titles include: "The History of Civilization," "In the Quest of the Images From Plutarch to Bryant," and "Seventh Grade and the Calyx of Modern Consciousness." "A careful account of one aspect of the teaching that goes on in . . . Rudolf Steiner schools." (*Commonweal*)

(102 pp)   0-88010-004-4 Paper

INTRODUCTION TO WALDORF EDUCATION *by Rudolf Steiner*
A short essay going to the heart of the Waldorf approach. Steiner explains the important changes occurring in the child at the 9th and 12th years and the way the curriculum meets these changes. It is probably the best short introduction to the development philosophy of Waldorf Education available. (This essay is contained in the forthcoming book *Renewal of the Social Organism.*)

(10 pp.)   0-88010-137-7 Paper

On Health and Therapy

THE ANTHROPOSOPHICAL APPROACH TO MEDICINE, VOL. 1
established by Friedrich Husemann, newly edited and revised by Otto Wolff, with contributions from eight others
This first volume of a projected four-volume medical text translated from the German and written out of the approach of Rudolf Steiner's anthroposophy will prove invaluable to medical practitioners seeking a concrete understanding of the body's relationship to soul and spirit. The readable text is also comprehensible to the interested layman. This volume includes an extensive section on developmental disorders and diseases of childhood and adolescence, followed by treatments of hysteria and neurasthenia, the polarities of inflammation and sclerosis, the biochemistry and pathology of nutrition and human metabolism, the pharmaceutical science of healing plants, and the "capillary-dynamic" and "sensitive crystallization" blood tests as diagnostic tools.

(414 pp., illus.)   0-88010-031-1 Cloth

BLESSED BY ILLNESS *by L.F.C. Mees*
"Illness is the embodiment of a deformation that otherwise might inhibit human evolution." This is only one of the many radical conclusions drawn by the Dutch physician, L.F.C. Mees, in this popular treatment of new medical ideas. Writing in an informal, conversational style, Dr. Mees offers

an alternative approach to today's "symptomatic medicine," which merely attempts to remove the nuisance of disease symptoms as quickly as possible. Instead, illness may be seen as a helper and problem-solver in life, and the medical doctor can assist this function through a new approach to therapy. An especially relevant section presents a novel study of cancer, urging the patient and physician to not merely fight the tumor but rather to "take over its task."

(220 pp.)   0-88010-054-0 Paper

CONCEPTION, BIRTH AND EARLY CHILDHOOD *by Norbert Glas*
Parents, teachers, physicians, nurses, and midwives looking for a more sensitive and spiritually aware approach to childbirth and rearing will find this book a wise and stimulating discussion. The dangers of anesthetics, artifical insemination, vaccination, nicotine, television, the playpen, and premature abstraction; the benefits of home-birth, mother-child bonding, breastfeeding, warmth and gentleness, natural surroundings, rhythmic repetition, and fairy tales—all these and many other subtler truths of pregnancy, childbirth, and early childhood that have only recently found a wider acceptance were authoritatively treated over 30 years ago in this timeless book by Dr. Glas.

(152 pp)   0-91014-254-8 Paper

Write for a free catalog of these and other books by Rudolf Steiner and related authors to:

Anthroposophic Press
Bell's Pond
Star Route
Hudson, NY 12534

DATE DUE

AUG 28 '97			
12-30-98			
11/11/00			
AP 12 '03			
SE 01 '03			
10/31/03			
NO 7 '04			
ILL			
1/13/11			
GAYLORD			PRINTED IN U.S.A.